30 Days
of Character Strengths

A Guided Practice to Ignite Your Best

by Jane S. Anderson

30 Days of Character Strengths:
A Guided Practice to Ignite Your Best

by Jane S. Anderson

Published by
Strength Based Living LLC

http://StrengthBasedLiving.com

Cover designed by Monica Rix Paxson, Relentlessly Creative

Edited by Kathryn Britton, Theano Coaching LLC

Praise for *30 Days of Character Strengths*

"With just the right mix of theory and practice, Jane Anderson has put together an accessible and rigorous strength-based guideline to both success and happiness. Day by day, this book will help you ignite what's best within you, your work and relationships."

> —Tal Ben-Shahar, PhD, Bestselling author of *Happier* and *The Joy of Leadership*, and founder of the Happiness Studies Academy

"To get and to give the most in your life, keep close at hand *30 Days of Character Strengths*. It presents important breakthrough discoveries in positive psychology at a much needed time, and in a well articulated, practical manner. Jane Anderson has given us a roadmap for developing new strength-based habits to improve our lives. Don't just read it…USE it!"

> —Donna Mayerson, PhD, Advisor for Applied Practice at the global non-profit VIA Institute on Character

"Ready for transformation? Give yourself the gift of a 30-day strengths practice in Jane Anderson's book *30 Days of Character Strengths*. Jane is a gentle and thorough guide who unlike most practitioners and scholars in positive psychology, digs wide and deep into the character strengths work, uncovering all the nooks and crannies of character strengths practices.

No longer can there be an excuse to not work with your strengths! As with meditation practices, people are quick to see the benefit of character strengths practices but slow to establish a daily practice routine. This book fills that gap. Follow Jane's lead and your strengths practice will be soaring by the end of the month!"

> —Ryan M. Niemiec, PsyD, Author of *Character Strengths Interventions: A Field Guide for Practitioners* and *Mindfulness and Character Strengths: A Practical Guide to Flourishing*, Education Director at the VIA Institute on Character

"In her own quest for excellence, Jane Anderson has completed more than forty 30-day practices and continues to promote positive habit formation. She has created a 30-day guide to help you incorporate awareness of character strengths into your own specific context, whether you need to advocate for your children, deal with difficult people, or feel more engaged at work. The activities in this workbook can help you turn knowledge into wisdom and practice into firm habits."

> —Kathryn H. Britton, Writing Mentor and Executive Coach, Co-Author of *Character Strengths Matter: How to Live a Full Life* and *Smarts and Stamina: The Busy Person's Guide to Optimal Health and Performance*

"*30 Days of Character Strengths* is an eminently practical book that achieves its aims: to help us explore our lives through a lens of strengths. Half-way through the book, I was thinking "I want to give this to my children" and highlighting what I wanted to try in my work with clients in therapy and coaching. Jane Anderson candidly shares her own personal and professional experiences and distills research findings to help us see how our goals, relationships, and all sorts of situations in everyday life can benefit from a strengths perspective.

With humor, kindness and creativity, the author helps readers establish a unique daily practice. I especially like how she invites us to reflect in writing, using very original writing prompts. By writing about ourselves from this perspective, we can develop personal narratives that are more inclusive of our strengths and can enrich our sense of who we are."

—Margarita Tarragona, PhD, author of *Positive Identities: Positive Psychology and Narrative Practices*

"Engaging your strengths each and every day has enormous benefits. Now, thanks to this fun and actionable book, you have a way to access and grow that superpower on a regular basis, tapping into the best within yourself. Get this book, use it, and uncover a greater capacity for goodness, living into more of who you already are."

—Megan McDonough, CEO and co-founder, Wholebeing Institute

"In clear, direct, inspiring style Jane Anderson provides a template for positive strength-based behavior change that not only enables any of us to build a more optimistic approach to daily living, she structures for us the opportunity to become our best selves. Research abounds about the value of leading from strengths in order to thrive and to manage difficult moments well. Through her elegant guidance, we are encouraged to elevate those qualities and virtues that bring our best self to the fore when we are in internal conflict, wrestling with difficult others, or conversely creating a happy home or building a dream. This work is for everyone: the manager who seeks to form a more effective team, the parent who wants to flood their home with efficacy and optimism, the adult who is ready for excellence, and the young adult who searches for balance and inspiration from within."

—Maria Sirois, PsyD, author of *A Short Course in Happiness After Loss (and Other Dark, Difficult Times)*

"In *30 Days of Character Strengths*, Jane Anderson provides an elegant approach to living deeply from your character strengths. You will experience a radical positive change in your self-understanding, elevate your own positivity and that of others, and begin expressing yourself fully and authentically. Her style and approach give me the feeling that I am on this 30-day journey with a friend and expert."

—Karen S. Whelan-Berry, PhD, Associate Professor at Springfield College, Manager of Research Development at Wholebeing Institute

"Jane Anderson's *30 Days of Character Strengths* is timely and important as it relates to developing character, elevating people to be their best, and contributing to the greater good. It is well written and user friendly in its balance of theory and practice. I heard her unique voice throughout—she is there every step of the way—encouraging and creating the way power to go deeper in our individual strengths journeys. This guided strengths practice can help anyone regardless of their familiarity with character strengths. I can't wait to share it with clients. If you wish to take the next step on your journey, this is the resource for you."

—Phoebe Atkinson, Psychotherapist, Faculty at Wholebeing Institute

Table of Contents

With Gratitude

I discovered something unexpected while writing this book: collaborating with others can transform a solo, sometimes isolating, journey into an energizing one. As someone high on the extrovert scale, I found this realization to be game changing. A community of brilliant friends, family, clients, and colleagues contributed their character strengths to this book, inspiring me to elevate mine and persevere to finish. Using a lens of strengths, I'd like to express my gratitude to them.

To my teachers, mentors, and coaches, from whom I continue to learn: Ryan Niemiec, Donna Mayerson, Tal Ben-Shahar, Megan McDonough, Maria Sirois, Kathryn Britton, Margarita Tarragona, Karen Whelan-Berry, and Phoebe Atkinson. Your love of learning is contagious. Your mastery and methods are impeccable. Thank you for the information and inspiration.

To my clients, colleagues, friends, and family who agreed to let me share their stories: your experiences are universal. Thank you for your bravery and for allowing others to learn from you.

To the volunteers who tested activities in this book or offered to read excerpts and provide feedback: John, Tunie, Jud, T, Donna S., Lori, Mary, Kathy, Nicole, Resa, Barbara, Kathleen, Phoebe, Karen, Alison, Jaci, Marni, Karissa, Sonja, and Laurel. Your curiosity, perspective, and kindness were the wind in my sails and helped me persevere to the finish. Thank you.

To my 30-day practice accountability group: Alison, Laurel, Dina, Brenda, Jaci, Toby, and Carol. We journeyed through over forty consecutive 30-day practices together. Your journeys were part of the inspiration for this book. Thank you for your perseverance, humor, and love along the way.

To my writing group: Cindy, Dwayne, Kristin, and Katharina. Your honesty, judgment, and perspective helped polish rough edges. Thank you.

To others on this journey: Sonja and the Wholebeing Institute (WBI) team; fellow teaching assistants for WBI's Certificate in Positive Psychology (CiPP) program (CiPP 3, 4, and California); participants in my study groups from CiPP 2, 3, 4, and California; all CiPPsters; VIA team members; and fellow participants in VIA's Mindfulness Based Strengths Practice course (1, 2, and 30-day practices). Thank you for the learning and growing together.

To my production team: Monica, Kathryn, and Julie. Thank you for sharing your creative talents and expertise. You know how to get things done.

To those who value me for who I am, with my quirky combination of creativity, humor, perspective, curiosity, and kindness: my family. John, Jud, Elizabeth, Matt, Mom, Sue, Terry, and Sarah, I thank you. John, you know better than anyone about the ups and downs of my writing journey. I send a heartfelt, special thanks to you.

I feel blessed to be in a community with all of you.

VIA Classification of Character Strengths and Virtues

The WISDOM Virtue

CREATIVITY Original, adaptive, ingenuity, seeing and doing things in different ways

CURIOSITY Interest, novelty-seeking, exploration, openness to experience

JUDGMENT Critical thinking, thinking through all sides, not jumping to conclusions

LOVE OF LEARNING Mastering new skills and topics, systematically adding to knowledge

PERSPECTIVE Wisdom, providing wise counsel, taking the big picture view

The COURAGE Virtue

BRAVERY Valor, not shrinking from threat or challenge, facing fears, speaking up for what's right

HONESTY Authenticity, being true to oneself, sincerity without pretense, integrity

PERSEVERANCE Persistence, industry, finishing what one starts, overcoming obstacles

ZEST Vitality, enthusiasm for life, vigor, energy, not doing things half-heartedly

The HUMANITY Virtue

LOVE Loving and being loved, valuing close relations with others, genuine warmth

KINDNESS Generosity, nurturance, care, compassion, altruism, doing for others

SOCIAL INTELLIGENCE Aware of motives and feelings of oneself and others, knows what makes others tick

The JUSTICE Virtue

FAIRNESS Adhering to principles of justice, not allowing feelings to bias decisions about others

LEADERSHIP Organizing group activities to get things done, positively influencing others

TEAMWORK Citizenship, social responsibility, loyalty, contributing to a group effort

The TEMPERANCE Virtue

FORGIVENESS Mercy, accepting others' shortcomings, giving people a second chance, letting go of hurt

HUMILITY Modesty, letting one's accomplishments speak for themselves

PRUDENCE Careful about one's choices, cautious, not taking undue risks

SELF-REGULATION Self-control, disciplined, managing impulses/emotions/vices

The TRANSCENDENCE Virtue

APPRECIATION OF BEAUTY & EXCELLENCE Awe and wonder for beauty, admiration for skill and moral greatness

GRATITUDE Thankful for the good, expressing thanks, feeling blessed

HOPE Optimism, positive future-mindedness, expecting the best and working to achieve it

HUMOR Playfulness, bringing smiles to others, lighthearted, seeing the lighter side

SPIRITUALITY Connecting with the sacred, purpose, meaning, faith, religiousness

BEFORE YOU BEGIN

Introduction

Suppose you had access to something that can change your work, relationships, health, and life in unimaginably positive ways. By its nature, it can energize you, increase your productivity, boost your confidence, and strengthen relationships.

It's not a drug. It doesn't require intensive physical exercise. You don't have to work harder to earn it. Its benefits are priceless, and it doesn't come with a price tag. Every person on the planet already has it, but not everyone fully uses it. Many of us don't even realize we have it . . . or why it matters.

"It" is your unique character strengths profile. The VIA Institute on Character, a non-profit organization based in Cincinnati, Ohio, dedicated to the research and practice of character strengths, defines character strengths as "...core capacities for thinking, feeling, and behaving in ways that can bring benefit to oneself and others."[1]

For example:

- Creativity: the spark that ignites design, building, and innovation.
- Bravery: the boldness of going into uncharted territory or standing up for someone who doesn't have a voice.

- Kindness: the connector that joins us in our humanity.
- Perseverance: the grit behind getting possible and impossible things done.

When a client wowed the management team, who subsequently agreed to fund her project, she engaged Creativity and Bravery. When a friend had a difficult but thoughtful conversation with his teenage daughter and she heeded his advice, he used Kindness and Perseverance. Fueled by their character strengths, my client and friend both felt exhilarated, energized, and unstoppable. One did a happy dance, fist pump, and the victory pose. The other yelled out loud, "Yes! *I did that!*"

Character strengths help define who you are and what you do when at your best.

Your character strengths are not only core capacities, they also *give you* capacity in both heroic and everyday moments like these.

In a world that frequently focuses on what's wrong, character strengths represent the opposite: what's good, what's strong, and what works within individuals, teams, families, communities, and organizations. Character strengths are one of the most researched topics in the field of positive psychology, the scientific study of human flourishing.

In a July 2017 conference presentation, I heard Martin E. P. Seligman, one of the founding fathers of positive psychology, say the following:

> "*The world is captivated by fixing what's wrong. But that only gets us to zero. The absence of ill-being does not equal well-being. The absence of bad relationships does not equal positive relationships. The absence of negative emotions does not equal positive emotions. There's something beyond that is worth pursuing. You must pursue the positive.*"

This book is about pursuing the positive through character strengths.

By building on what's strong, not just fixing what's wrong, we take what's best in ourselves and others and amplify that to cultivate the good. In a 2012 article David Cooperrider, pioneer in Appreciative Inquiry, a way of harnessing what's best in people and organizations, articulates a concentration effect of strengths. He says that strengths do more than perform…they *transform* and help us magnify "what is best" and imagine "what is next" in order to create upward momentum.[2]

Magnifying what's best to create upward momentum takes many shapes and forms. For instance, my entrepreneurial partner in life is passionate about buying fledgling businesses, rejuvenating them, and returning them to the owners in much better shape than he found them. He attributes much of his success to not only finding the right opportunities, but also negotiating the right deals. That's where his signature strength, Fairness, comes in.

> Pursuing the positive in life is a worthy and essential pursuit.

He says, "It's not worth pursuing a deal that doesn't have something for everyone. A fair deal is a right deal. It benefits all parties and thus has lasting value and sustainability." His successful track record certainly bears that out.

On a personal note, after my dad passed away following a heroic eight-year battle with late-stage cancer, I struggled for days to form the message I would deliver at his memorial service. When I thought about who he was at his best and his character strengths, it suddenly became easy.

I highlighted Perseverance, Love of Learning, and Judgment, his top three, and shared a brief story about each of these strengths in action during his life. It was an authentic, meaningful way for me to honor my dad, and it connected us together as others shared their own memories of him at his best.

When individuals on a team build on each other's strengths, the result can be transformational. Think of your favorite musical groups combining their strengths and talents to perform your favorite song. They create something entirely new beyond the original, as in the striking blues duet by pop star Justin Timberlake and country star Chris Stapleton at the 2015 Country Music Awards (at https://tinyurl.com/blues-duet).

In each of these examples, strengths did more than perform. They transformed and created upward momentum through performance, positive connections, and enhanced well-being.

Engaging strengths can lead to enhanced well-being, transformation, and new possibilities.

A few phrases I've heard others use to describe living with a character strengths focus are:

- Living deeply,
- Touching life,
- Living out loud,
- Expressing yourself unapologetically for who you are,
- Life altering, and
- Being in the zone of greatness.

Think about your own positive contributions to a relationship, a project you're working on, or a special moment in time. The relationships you cultivate, accomplishments you achieve, and happiness you feel in life are all due, at least in part, to your character strengths. Although life hands out stress, loss, and illness, your character strengths are there to help you manage adversity.

Whether you're engaging your character strengths *well,* or as often as you might, is another matter. Many of us don't have a meaningful awareness of our character strengths or understand how to cultivate them. I didn't when I began my own strengths journey many years ago. I was unable to see myself through a lens of strengths, although I was great at pinpointing and fixing what could be improved.

There isn't anything wrong with that, but I felt depleted as I worked harder to improve my relationships, work, and health. It seemed like I was simultaneously applying the gas pedal and the brake, creating friction and not getting where I wanted to go.

Some of us believe it's better to focus on weaknesses rather than build on strengths, even though research shows the opposite is true. Ignoring weaknesses doesn't seem prudent, but they typically attract plenty of time and resources. Consider the multi-billion-dollar consulting industry, much of which focuses on fixing problems and shoring up gaps.

Living your strengths is an ongoing journey of discovery and growth.

This book is for everyone who wishes to live more deeply and enter the zone of greatness. Cultivating your character strengths can be your pathway to learning, growth, and transformation.

If you're new to character strengths, you might wonder what they are, how to identify them, why you should invest in them, or how to get started. This book will answer those questions and many more. It will guide you through thirty days of activities to help you cultivate your strengths.

If you're experienced with character strengths, you might already know how to identify and engage them. Or perhaps you can spot strengths easily within yourself or others. Although these practices are foundational, this book will help you dive into other facets of character strengths.

You'll engage strengths to achieve an important goal, resolve a conflict, and soothe yourself after making a mistake. You'll discover how overusing and underusing your strengths impacts relationships and outcomes. You'll practice engaging strengths in a balanced, perhaps even optimal, way. You'll use your strengths to shift a bad habit into a positive one.

If you're a parent or grandparent, a leader or manager, a teacher, consultant, coach, therapist, or other professional who is passionate about bringing out the best in others, this book provides thirty days of inspiration, including information, stories, research-based activities, and resources to share with your kids, employees, students, and clients.

Consider this: from Socrates to present day leadership experts, one of the principles of great leadership is to "know thyself." To that end, I invite you to think about investing in your own strengths journey.

Allowing strengths to matter is an essential role for leaders of families, social groups, teams, communities, and organizations.

After the devastating terrorist attack on the World Trade Center buildings in New York City in 2001, Martin Seligman and Christopher Peterson, Seligman's esteemed partner in pioneering the character strengths work, described character strengths as traits that help us rise to the occasion. Then they delivered a call to action:

> *"As individuals, we need to look within ourselves to identify the signature strengths we already possess. As members of groups and organizations, especially if we are in positions of leadership and influence, we need to do everything possible to arrange situations to allow the signature strengths of individuals to matter."* [3]

Over a decade and a half later, we have even more opportunities to rise to the occasion due to devastating *and* inspirational events. Whether you're new to character strengths or an experienced practitioner, I hope you'll join me in pursuing the positive by cultivating strengths.

What are Character Strengths and Why Do They Matter?

"Strengths have been found to predict well-being...and have been linked to increased happiness, well-being, work satisfaction, work engagement, meaning, self-efficacy, self-esteem, goal achievement, positive affect, vitality, and lower perceived stress."

—A summary of research findings by Ryan M. Niemiec, author and Education Director at the VIA Institute on Character[4]

Character strengths are an expression of goodness in people around the globe.

For over 2,000 years we humans have catalogued what's wrong with us. Current systems include the *Diagnostic and Statistical Manual of Mental Disorders* and the *International Classification of Diseases.* They capture the known range of mental and physical disorders used for medical diagnoses and treatment.

Recently, scientists have widened the perspective to include what's strong. What is right and good in people? How can we cultivate these best qualities? How do they differ among cultures?

To answer these questions Seligman and Peterson, with support from the Mayerson Foundation, an organization dedicated to creating caring communities, led a team of dozens of scientists for three years. They reviewed hundreds of articles across religions, geographic locations, and time, and studied different cultures around the globe.

Their project resulted in the groundbreaking publication *Character Strengths and Virtues: A Handbook and Classification.* It offers a framework for identifying, measuring, and cultivating human strengths. Among the 24 character strengths are Curiosity, Fairness, Perspective, Judgment, and Love. Notice that the character strengths names are capitalized throughout this book, making it easy to recognize them. The strengths are organized within six virtues including wisdom, courage and justice. You can find the entire classification of character strengths and virtues at the beginning of this book.

The research on character strengths is robust and continues to grow. It explores the benefits of expressing strengths in key domains such as the workplace, at home, in academic and social settings, when taking care of our health . . . in virtually all parts of life.

Character strengths can be pathways to what matters most in life, such as satisfying work and relationships, achievement, and well-being.

The opening quotation in this chapter highlights many positive outcomes you can experience by engaging character strengths. Consider, also, the following research findings:

- **In organizations,** using character strengths is connected with not only job satisfaction but also productivity and organizational citizenship behavior. These connections are explained by high positive emotions and engagement, according to a 2016 workplace study.[5]

- **In education,** character strengths of the mind (e.g., self-regulation, perseverance, love of learning) were predictive of school success, according to a 2012 study of 12-year-olds in the classroom.[6]

- **For caretakers of children with disabilities,** a pilot strengths-focused group…for caretakers of children with cerebral palsy found significantly lower parent stress and higher hope at the conclusion of the group and at 1-month follow-up, according to a team of researchers.[7]

These findings seem astonishing individually, but they're even more astonishing collectively. You can review hundreds of research findings on the VIA Institute's website (at https://tinyurl.com/VIA-research-findings).

Over five million people have taken the survey worldwide. They're probably like you and me, seeking ways to bring forth who they are and what they do when at their best, and passionate about bringing out the best in others.

Bringing forth our best isn't always intuitive or easy. In the next section, you'll explore common roadblocks and how to unblock them in order to fuel your work, your relationships, and yourself with strengths.

Common Roadblocks

Cultivating your strengths and helping others cultivate theirs is a journey of exploration and practice. As with other worthwhile journeys in life, you're bound to run into roadblocks that can curtail momentum. These roadblocks include:

- A negativity bias
- A lack of awareness and other forms of strengths blindness
- The autopilot mind

One of the most difficult roadblocks to overcome is our inherent negativity bias. This negativity bias refers to the fact that we pay more attention to negative experiences than to positive ones. This human tendency probably evolved to help us respond rapidly to threats.

If I were to say one negative and ten positive things about you, you'd be most likely to remember the negative one. Dr. Rick Hanson, Senior Fellow of the Greater Good Science Center at UC Berkeley, says that "…the brain is like Velcro® for negative experiences but Teflon™ for positive ones."[8]

If you're not convinced this applies to you, think about your last family dinner or team meeting. Did it focus primarily on what was going well or what wasn't? Try it for yourself. The next time you see friends, colleagues, or family mem-

Cultivating strengths isn't always easy or intuitive. Understanding and managing roadblocks you might encounter along the way can help you stay on track.

bers, ask "What's going well?" They're likely to respond with discomfort, a pause to ponder the question, or avoidance of the question altogether.

It's a bit like trying to fold your arms in the opposite way. We're simply not accustomed to thinking and behaving from a position of what's strong. Roy F. Baumeister and colleagues wrote a prominent psychology paper stating that "bad is stronger than good."[9] This bias unwittingly keeps our attention focused on what's wrong: self-criticism, disapproval, disappointments, problems, and difficulty.

Cultivating your strengths will help you shift the negativity bias and pursue the positive.

The second roadblock is lack of awareness. If I asked you to name your top strengths, would you be able to? If not, you're in good company. Many of us don't have a meaningful awareness of our strengths. Some of us can't name them or notice when they're in action. Others don't value their strengths or understand how they become pathways to excellence and well-being.

This book will help you explore your strengths, develop a more meaningful awareness of them, and discover how they become your pathways to positive outcomes. It will help you learn how to use them to just the right degree, neither underusing them nor overusing them.

A final roadblock is something we all grapple with: the autopilot mind. The autopilot mind is a byproduct of our busy culture. As we multi-task and try to accomplish more in less time, the autopilot mind flies us deeper into mindlessness. We become less aware of what we're doing, what we're thinking, how we're feeling, and how we impact others.

This book will help you pause and tune into your best self, even in life's difficult situations.

Are you ready to begin? You're almost there.

> Your character strengths can help you navigate virtually all situations you face each day.

Getting the Most from This Book

"Change does not happen because we wish it or because the universe magically aligns to make it so. It occurs when we make the conscious choice to imagine a better future and then choose the steps that bring us to that very future."

—Maria Sirois, author of *A Short Course in Happiness After Loss (and Other Dark, Difficult Times),* Director of Curriculum at Wholebeing Institute

Creating lasting change can be achieved through positive habit formation and practice.

If you desire to live more authentically and fully, even just five or ten percent more, it's not likely to happen by simply wishing for it. You need to create habits to support your desired outcomes.

This book is a guided strengths practice designed to help you create strengths-based habits - ways of thinking, feeling, and behaving. It offers thirty different activities, many of which take as little as ten minutes. It weaves together weekly themes and stories with daily activities and reflection questions.

Weekly Themes

Week 1 – Exploring Your Best Self (Understanding Your Strengths)

Week 2 – Connecting & Building Relationships (Strengths-Spotting)

Week 3 – Boosting Confidence & Competence (Developing Strengths)

Week 4 – Living Your Strengths (Doing More of What You Do Best)

Closing Days – Celebrating Best Moments and Crafting a Future Fueled by Strengths

Reflection and repetition help to consolidate your learning.

Daily Activities and Reflections

Many of the activities in this book are based on research. I use them in my life. My colleagues, clients, family, and friends use many of them in theirs. By investing a small amount of time in these daily activities, you will:

- develop a more confident and meaningful awareness of your strengths,
- acknowledge, appreciate, and value your strengths and the strengths you see in others,
- integrate your strengths into daily activities, and
- craft a future shaped by strengths.

At the end of each daily activity, I offer a reflection question to help consolidate your learning.

Why 30 Days?

Recent breakthroughs in the field of neuroscience, the scientific study of the nervous system, shine a light on how habits are formed in the brain. One key to forming habits is repetition. Experts use a sledding metaphor to explain this.

> *"When we go down the hill on a sled… we have the option of taking different paths through the soft snow each time. But should we choose the same path a second or third time, tracks will start to develop…and neural circuits, once established, tend to become self-sustaining."*

—Norman Doidge, author of *The Brain That Changes Itself*[10]

In other words, through the repetition of positive thoughts, emotions, and actions, we create positive self-sustaining neural circuits that drive habits.

William James, psychologist and philosopher, knew long before the field of neuroscience was born that it takes about 21 days to begin forming a new habit. A more recent study on habit formation shows that it can take longer, on average about 66 days.[11]

How much time it will take *you* to form a habit grounded in strengths depends. It might take 15 days or 66 days or somewhere in between. After thirty days of consistent practice though, even just a little bit each day, you should see and feel a shift in your thoughts, emotions, and actions as you pursue the positive more often.

Be patient with yourself as you begin or deepen your strengths practice.

In the past three plus years, I completed over forty consecutive 30-day practices. With a small group of like-minded colleagues, I continue to cultivate positive habits using this approach. As a result, we are enjoying new hobbies, exercising more, completing meaningful projects, and improving relationships. We've discovered new things about ourselves, and we've used strengths to cultivate goodness, happiness, and success. I hope you will, too.

Tips to Help You Succeed

1. Tailor your practice to what works for you. You might challenge yourself and decide to complete 30 consecutive days. You might make it a 60-day practice, completing the activity one day and the reflection question the next. If you're familiar with character strengths, you might choose the activities that are new to you. Ideally, complete each week's activities in chronological order because they become progressively more complex.

2. If possible, stay consistent by maintaining a regular schedule. Schedule the time in your daily routine and remind yourself to practice using well-placed sticky notes or an alert on your phone.

Set yourself up for success by following these tips.

3. Return to your practice when you miss a day. Life intervenes, schedules shift, commitment wanes. Give yourself permission to be human, and simply return to your practice. Sometimes *this* is the practice.

4. Stay flexible and open. Try to stay open to any activities that do not at first resonate with you and the situations you face. If you feel stuck, feel free to move on and come back to the activity later.

5. Work with an accountability partner. Buddy up with a trusted friend, colleague, or family member. Work with a strengths-knowledgeable professional. Research shows that having an accountability buddy significantly boosts the likelihood of success in change efforts.[12,13]

6. Celebrate your progress, not just accomplishments. Pat yourself on the back when you have an insight, try something new, go outside your comfort zone, catch yourself on autopilot, or shift away from your negativity bias. Dance, sing, shout out, *"I did that!"* Yes, you did.

7. Notice that the first letter of each strength is capitalized when mentioned throughout the book. This will help you recognize the 24 character strengths easily as you complete each day.

8. Use your strengths! Prudence will help you plan and schedule practice time. Zest will help you move into action. Humor will help you enjoy yourself along the way. Self-regulation will help you return to your practice when you skip a few days. Perseverance will help you finish. All 24 character strengths can help you navigate the roadblocks and complete your practice.

What You Need to Get Started

Getting started is easy. You'll need:

- This book
- Internet access
- A journal (physical journal, laptop, app, or whatever method you prefer to record your experiences).

Feel free to make notes in the margins on each page.

I'm excited for you as you begin your journey fueled by Bravery, Hope, Perseverance, Humor, Gratitude, Zest, and 18 other character strengths.

Let's get started!

Ready? Here we go!

WEEK

1

Exploring Your Best Self (Understanding Your Strengths)

> *"Make the most of yourself…for that is all there is of you."*
>
> —Ralph Waldo Emerson

Welcome to Week 1!

Can you recall a time when you contributed everything you had to offer, accomplished everything you wanted, or expressed yourself authentically without feeling a need to impress others? Maybe you were entertaining friends, doing a great job on a project, or raising money for a worthy cause.

If an example doesn't readily come to mind, I invite you to reflect on an everyday moment when you felt confident, content, or energized. It could be when you were playing with your kids and felt happy. Or when you stood up to your boss and felt Brave.

When you're in this zone, your unique profile of character strengths is engaged, helping you express who you are and what you do best. When engaging your strengths, you might have a sense of being unstoppable. You might feel understood or valued. You might notice a boost in energy and positive emotions.

This week's activities provide a framework to identify and explore your unique profile of character strengths. The activities will help you:

- Deepen your understanding of who you are and what you do when at your best
- Connect your character strengths with positive outcomes

Enjoy the week!

Day 1

Discover something new about character

Your first activity is to take the free VIA survey to identify your unique character strengths profile.

Today's Activity

1. If you're new to character strengths, take the free VIA survey on the VIA Institute website (http://www. viacharacter.org/www/Character-Strengths-Survey). It takes about 15 minutes to complete. If you're not new to character strengths and haven't updated your results in over a year, feel free to retake the survey.

2. After completing the survey, you will receive a ranked list of 24 strengths online. This is your unique character strengths profile. Print a copy of your profile and really take it in. Read the definitions and explore wherever your mind takes you. You'll access this profile over and over again, so keep it in a convenient place.

3. Feel free to browse the treasure trove of resources offered on the VIA site. Be sure to check out a short video called *The Science of Character* and a graphic of the VIA Classification of Character Strengths and Virtues, available for downloading and printing. You can find them at http://www.viacharacter.org/www/ Character-Strengths. For your convenience, the VIA Classification of Character Strengths and Virtues is also included at the beginning of this book.

Your profile of character strengths is unique to you. It is highly unlikely that you will ever meet anyone with exactly the same profile.

Today's Reflection and Writing Prompt

Today I discovered that…

Complete this reflection following your practice or at the end of the day. It's an incomplete sentence for you to journal about. Perhaps you discovered that your results feel spot on. Or maybe something was confusing or disappointing. Perhaps you discovered something else altogether.

Don't evaluate your writing or worry about punctuation, grammar, contradictions, or things that don't make sense right now. Write whatever comes to mind, letting it flow through you and onto paper, your laptop, or the white space in this book.

If helpful, re-read what you wrote and highlight anything that resonates or stands out. This makes it easier to review your reflections later if you decide to return to them.

Day 2

Notice a signature strength

This week's quotation by Ralph Waldo Emerson is a call to action.

> *"Make the most of yourself…for that is all there is of you."*

It's about *cultivating who you already are:* your best, unique, and maybe even quirky qualities, even if that doesn't strictly align with who you think you should be, what others want from you, or what's happening around you.

Whether you're working toward a meaningful goal or dealing with a crisis, expressing your best self more often and intentionally is everything you or anyone else can expect from you. It's enough. "That is all there is of you."

This is where your signature strengths come into play. Your signature strengths help answer the question: What defines the essence of me and conveys who I am at my best?

In his book *Flourish,* Martin Seligman[1] describes the hallmarks of signature strengths as:

- A sense of ownership and authenticity ("This is the real me.")
- A feeling of excitement when using them
- A rapid learning curve
- A sense of yearning to find new ways to use them
- A feeling of inevitability ("Try to stop me.")
- Invigoration rather than exhaustion
- The creation and pursuit of projects that revolve around them
- Joy, zest, enthusiasm, even ecstasy

Your signature strengths express who you are and what you do when at your best.

33

A large and expanding body of research on signature strengths informs how to develop strengths to benefit oneself and other people.

Your signature strengths naturally infuse your work, relationships, and health with energy and positive emotions. They boost your capacity to achieve goals, solve problems, find meaning and engagement, build close relationships, and enhance your mental and physical health.

Engaging your signature strengths more often and in new ways is one of your biggest growth opportunities. Consider the following research findings that speak to signature strengths' impacts on a wide range of life domains, such as:

Work, where many of us spend a majority of our time. In a three-year thematic analysis of drivers of employee engagement, focusing on character strengths was among the three most crucial drivers (along with managing emotions and aligning purpose). Specifically, employees are encouraged to identify, use, and alert others of their signature strengths as well as converse with managers about strengths use opportunities in the organization, according to a 2011 study about employee engagement.[2]

Raising and educating our youth, who will become future leaders. Among youth, the use of signature strengths in novel ways along with personally meaningful goal-setting led to increases in student engagement and hope, from a 2011 pilot study of strength-based coaching for primary school students.[3]

Personal well-being. There is a strong connection between well-being and the use of signature strengths because strengths help us make progress on our goals and meet our basic needs for independence, relationship, and competence, from a 2010 study evaluating the effect of signature strengths on the pursuit of goals.[4]

Also, using one's signature strengths in a new way increased happiness and decreased depression for 6 months, per a 2012 study on strength-based positive interventions.[5]

The topic of strengths is one of the most researched in positive psychology. The body of research continues to inform the development and application of strengths in different domains: the workplace, academia, home life, health, relationships, and others.

It's natural to want to engage your strengths more often. One of the most fruitful things you can do, however, is explore how you already express your signature strengths. This will help you understand how they lead to the outcomes you desire.

For example, as I write this page I notice I'm using my signature strength Creativity to weave together inspiration and information on this topic of signature strengths. Tonight, I'll use Creativity to create a delicious and nutritious dinner using a few ingredients from the fridge and pantry. I feel good about using my Creativity in service of feeding my family well without being wasteful. We appreciate our time together as we enjoy a tasty meal.

Earlier today, I used Creativity to help a client brainstorm solutions to a problem he faced. He appreciated the wider array of options we generated. This collaboration strengthened our relationship.

In fact, I notice many ways I express Creativity: my approach to working with clients, the design for my home renovation, and the personalized gift I chose for my neighbor. This signature strength influences much of what I do throughout the day. It leads to connection, collaboration, excellence, and other positive outcomes.

Now it's your turn to notice when you express one of your signature strengths and how it leads you to positive outcomes.

Signature strengths can become pathways to what we value in life, like positive relationships and excellence.

Today's Activity

1. Check out this video of leaders in positive psychology who name their own signature strengths (at https://tinyurl.com/leader-strengths). Notice their energy and the language they use.

2. Review the top 7 or 8 character strengths on your VIA survey results, and choose one that resonates as a signature strength.

3. Think of examples when you used this strength. Try to come up with examples in all key parts of your life, for example, at work, at home, in your social life, managing your health, or keeping up with daily routines.

4. Imagine how this strength contributes to the good in your life. How do you feel when using it? What positive outcomes does it enable?

5. Record your examples and answers so that you can review them later.

Today's Reflection and Writing Prompt

The strength I chose resonates as a signature strength because…

Perhaps you noticed how your strength helped you achieve a goal, connect with others, boost your confidence, or solve a problem. Or perhaps you recognized some of the many hallmarks of signature strengths.

Remember to let the words flow without evaluating your writing or worrying about punctuation, grammar, and contradictions. If helpful, re-read what you wrote and highlight anything that stands out.

Day 3

Imagine life without a signature strength

For several years, I had the honor of supporting Ryan Niemiec and Donna Mayerson, both of the VIA Institute on Character, in an online course about integrating mindfulness and character strengths practices in coaching contexts. The course was offered by Wholebeing Institute, an educational organization co-founded by Tal Ben-Shahar, best-selling author of *Happier* and *The Joy of Leadership*, and Megan McDonough, CEO.

Among the many activities they introduced, one was a game-changer for understanding signature strengths. First, we were asked to choose one of our signature strengths and describe its importance in our lives. Next, we imagined life without that strength. Finally, we were asked to name a word or short phrase to describe what we imagined. This activity is so profound that I've used it often with others.

One of my client's top strengths was Hope. She was able to identify many examples of expressing Hope at work, home, with friends, and even in daily activities. She wasn't quite clear, however, about why Hope was extraordinary or how it helped define her positive identity.

Then she completed this activity. Afterwards, she described life without Hope like this:

- My outlook can't be positive. I can't feel optimistic about my future work, my kids growing up, my community, or country.

- I can only notice difficult events and negative expectations, not positive ones.

- I don't believe things can improve or change for the better.

Imagining life without signature strengths highlights their importance in daily life.

The words she used to describe the life she imagined? Empty. Helpless. Lifeless.

One workshop participant chose Love. He couldn't connect with others in a warm and friendly way. He wouldn't be able to feel or value close relationships at work, at home, or with friends. There would be no hugging and kissing. He described this world as unimaginable.

This activity helps us imagine what life would be like and what *we* would be like. Most of the time, it's not a picture we wish to paint for ourselves.

It might be difficult to appreciate how essential your signature strengths are until you think about life without them. Since this activity can leave you in a negative frame of mind, I've added a second reflection and writing prompt that will help you end on a positive note.

> Your signature strengths contribute to living life with integrity, purpose, and satisfaction.

Today's Activity*

1. Remind yourself of the signature strength you chose on Day 2. If you prefer, choose a different one. Notice how this strength is important to you. How do you use it to create excellence, solve problems, have fun, or achieve goals?

2. Next, imagine you're not allowed to use this strength for the next month. What would that be like? How would that feel?

   a. If you chose Fairness, there's no such thing as equality. You can't reason things out. You have no rights or responsibilities.

   b. If you chose Curiosity, you can't try new foods or ask questions. There's no novelty. You can't go exploring.

   c. If you chose Judgment, you can't analyze problems. There's no logic. You can't think about important details because there aren't any.

     d. If you chose Honesty, you can't have integrity.
       There's no valuing the truth. There's no "real you."

3. Write down a word or phrase that describes the picture you just painted about your life.

Today's Reflection and Writing Prompts

1. If the signature strength I chose didn't exist in my life…

2. Since this signature strength does exist in my life…

Complete these reflections following your practice or at the end of the day. Remember not to judge the writing as you go. Just let it flow.

*Based on Character Strength Intervention (CSI) 5 in *Character Strengths Interventions: A Field Guide for Practitioners* by Ryan Niemiec.

Day 4

Explore a strength that doesn't resonate

When I first took the VIA survey, I felt excited. My #1 strength, Creativity, felt like a natural fit and described me at my best. I could easily recall examples of expressing that strength. On Day 2, I mentioned how I use Creativity in my personal and professional lives. My brand of Creativity is less about creating art, the way artists and musicians do, and more about finding novel ways to do things. Creativity felt right at #1.

I landed on Humor at #2, but I didn't think of Humor as a strength. I was more interested in knowing where Leadership was. At the time, I viewed Leadership as a more desirable strength. There it was . . . way down at #16. Ouch – disappointing. I wondered how Humor could be #2 and Leadership #16.

Then I flipped to the last page and quickly noticed #24: Self-regulation. Definitely needed to work on that! I had other strong reactions, positive and negative, to my ranked list of character strengths.

By the end of my review, l felt slightly deflated about me at my best. I wanted to use my strengths more often, but I wasn't sure which were truly strengths or how to begin. I didn't realize all 24, even the lower ones, are strengths and not weaknesses. Many people I work with have similar reactions.

The VIA Institute on Character offers a simple 3-step framework for engaging strengths:

1. Become aware
2. Explore
3. Apply

The VIA survey results often surprise people. You might experience an unexpected but normal array of reactions ranging from disappointment to excitement.

The first step involves naming and recognizing your strengths. The second involves understanding how you express them. The third involves putting your strengths into action more intentionally. You can learn more about this framework on the VIA website (https://tinyurl.com/VIA-model).

It's natural to want to jump ahead to apply. That's where the excitement of engaging your strengths more often and in new ways comes in. Instead, I invite you to explore your reactions to your survey results and be open to potential blind spots.

Blind spots can hinder the journey to what's strong. Clearly, I had a blind spot around Humor. I neither saw Humor as a strength nor recognized it as part of my positive identity.

> Opening up to new perspectives is an important part of your strengths exploration.

A trusted colleague suggested I explore Humor, so I did. I noticed how I used Humor to connect with clients, family, and friends in a light-hearted way. I broke the ice with new acquaintances at networking events and joked with the bagger at the grocery store. I lightened heavy discussions with colleagues.

I realized how naturally I express Humor in different settings and how it opens the door to deeper relationships. I took my Humor practice to the next level and found funny YouTube videos like laughing quadruplets (https://tinyurl.com/laughing-quadruplets), watched my favorite improv TV show *Whose Line Is It Anyway?*, and recorded how often I laughed and felt playful. I told jokes and found ways to have fun and spend time with witty people.

I also found research that explained how Humor is a pathway to excellence, well-being, and strong relationships. Consider the following findings:

- According to a 2014 *Harvard Business Review* article about humor in the workplace, laughter "...relieves stress and boredom, boosts engagement and well-being, and spurs not only creativity and collaboration but also analytic precision and productivity."[6]

- A 2011 study on humor and pain says that laughter releases endorphins (feel-good chemicals in our bodies), which raise our ability to handle pain.[7]

- In terms of happiness, a 2016 trial of humor-based interventions showed that writing about 3 funny things that happened each day plus accompanying emotions boosted happiness for six months.[8]

I finally understood why I need light-heartedness and fun, especially when life becomes serious. It's who I am.

You don't need to explore your strengths to the extent I did, but notice how beneficial exploring can be. It's not unusual to see an array of emotions like excitement, surprise, disappointment, confusion, and pride in response to survey results. What came up for you when reviewing yours?

Today's Activity

1. Review your VIA survey results and the reflection you wrote on Day 1. Choose one character strength that doesn't particularly resonate with you. Perhaps you're Curious or skeptical about its value as a strength. Perhaps you wonder whether it's part of your core identity.

2.   Find the character strength you chose at http://www.
     viacharacter.org/www/CharacterStrengths/Sci-
     ence-Of-Character. Read the description and ways
     to cultivate it. Watch the video and review the movie
     and song titles.

3.   Now widen your perspective. Think of a time when
     you used this strength to accomplish something or
     connect with someone important to you. Write down
     examples of when you engaged this strength.

4.   Complete today's practice with one character strength.
     Then, if you choose, feel free to explore others.

Today's Reflection and Writing Prompt

When I delved into a particular character strength, I was
surprised by...

Day 5

Explore a strength you identify as phasic

Your phasic strengths are strengths you call forth strongly in certain situations to help you rise to the occasion.

This week I was meeting with a client, a small business owner. During the meeting, she spoke of a character strength she wanted to explore. At #14, Appreciation of Beauty and Excellence was a middle strength for her. Many people think of this strength as appreciating physical beauty, as in art or nature. She connected this strength with business outcomes.

She viewed running her business as part art, part science. Where there was complexity, she created simplicity. Where there were problems, she cultivated excellence, quality, and personal connection. She loved seeing a good plan, some skill, and hard work come together to benefit her customers, employees, and business. She engaged this strength to create simplicity and excellence.

For this client, the Appreciation of Beauty and Excellence is a *phasic strength*. Phasic strengths "...rise and fall according to the demands of specifiable situations," as defined in the *Character Strengths and Virtues* handbook.[9] In other words, we call them forth strongly when the situation calls for it.

Bravery is a strength often noted as phasic. Firefighters use Bravery to save people from burning buildings, but not when they're back at the fire station cooking dinner. You might use Bravery when standing up for someone without a voice or when helping a loved one in trouble, but not necessarily throughout the day.

For some, Bravery might be a signature strength, engaged frequently and easily across all domains. If Bravery is your signature strength, you will notice lower ranked strengths that are phasic. Ryan Niemiec has noted that phasic strengths are not signature strengths and therefore come from the middle or lower portion of your ranked list.[10]

One of my phasic strengths is Prudence at #22. Although it's a lower strength and I tend to be flexible and spontaneous in many parts of my life, I call this strength forth quite strongly in my work. My professional role requires me to make decisions, use resources wisely, and get things done. When I run work team meetings, I create an agenda, tell participants how they can best prepare, manage the time closely, and take other steps to ensure it goes smoothly. This is Prudence in action.

When do you rise to the occasion in your personal or professional life? Which strength helps you do so? Perhaps when spending time with friends, the kids, or grandkids, you express Humor and playfulness strongly, but you wouldn't think of it in other situations. Perhaps when working on certain projects or in your volunteer role you feel Zesty and enthusiastic, but you wouldn't describe yourself that way most of the time.

Today you'll explore the middle or lower part of your ranked list, noticing a strength you tend to call forth strongly to rise to the occasion.

Phasic strengths tend to come from the middle or lower third of your profile.

Today's Activity

1. Review your middle and lower strengths. Identify one that resonates as phasic.

2. Think of situations when you called forth this strength strongly. Recall how this strength contributed to your success or that of your team or family.

Today's Reflection and Writing Prompt

A phasic strength benefits me and other people when…

Day 6

Bring balance to your strengths

As you go about your daily life, you probably face countless situations in different settings. Each situation is unique. Even routine situations vary based on who you encounter, how you feel, and what you do.

How aware are you of using your character strengths in these different situations? Pause right now and ask yourself: What was I doing before I began today's activity? What strength was I using? How much of this strength was needed, given the situation? This last question speaks to one of the most important aspects of character strengths: engaging them in a balanced way.

The situations you encounter each day require different degrees of strengths expression.

Periodically, my family gets together to celebrate holidays and birthdays. We live in different states and lead full lives, so we don't have many opportunities to connect in person. Naturally, when we get together, we ask lots of questions about work, families, and friends to reconnect.

Curiosity is a signature strength for many of us. Engaging Curiosity in a balanced way ensures a pleasant sense of harmony as we catch up. However, when one Curious person slips into overdrive, the other ends up in the hot seat.

Hot seat is a term my kids created to describe their experience of Curiosity in overdrive. According to them, being in the hot seat is not pleasant. The questions become way too personal for comfort. They perceive the overly Curious person as nosy and no longer pleasantly interested. They feel like the subject of an interrogation, uncomfortable and resistant. Not exactly a relationship booster!

The Curious person in overdrive doesn't intend to create tension and stress. That's just a byproduct of asking too many questions of someone who isn't receptive. When *I'm* the overly Curious person, I know that's not me at my best with someone I care about.

On the flipside, if no one asked any questions we would seem uninterested in one another. When I fail to inquire about someone I care about, I'm also not at my best. I feel disappointed about missing a prime opportunity to connect with someone important to me.

> *"Too much (overuse) and too little (underuse) of character strengths use can have a negative impact on well-being and other important factors"*
>
> —Adam Grant and Barry Schwartz[11]

Suppose you're in an important networking meeting. If you underuse Curiosity, your networking partner might perceive you as uninterested, and you're less likely to establish a productive relationship. If you overuse Curiosity, she might perceive you as overly aggressive, and your chances of collaborating diminish. What's needed is the right amount for the situation.

Picture a continuum. In the middle is the balanced or optimal expression of each character strength. On one end of the continuum is overuse; on the other, underuse. The point in the middle is a matter of Judgment. For example, one of my friends experiences the hot seat much sooner than another. I try to adjust my Curiosity to meet each person's sensitivity.

Teamwork expressed in a balanced way is collaborative and participatory and leads to engagement, one of three key drivers of individual and organizational performance, according to a 2011 study about employee engagement.[12] Overuse of Teamwork might result in a team member over-relying on others and not pulling his weight. Underuse is common when a team member feels she can more efficiently accomplish a task independently, thus bypassing the team.

Expressing strengths in a balanced way, without underusing or overusing them, helps to create harmony within you, in your relationships, and at work.

Optimally engaging your character strengths leads you to closer relationships, personal well-being, and other positive outcomes. Overusing and underusing a strength can create conflict, stress, even suffering, and bring out your darker side rather than your authentic, positive qualities.

Fortunately, you can learn to manage overused and underused strengths and practice expressing them in a balanced way. You'll do this in Week 3. Today's activity is about simply exploring one of your signature strengths through the lens of balance, overuse, and underuse.

Today's Activity

1. Choose a signature strength to explore.

2. For the strength you chose, review the description of its overuse and underuse on the Character Strengths Overuse and Underuse worksheet located at the back of this book.

3. Think of an example when you used this strength. Did you use it in a balanced way? In other words, was it the right amount for the situation?

4. Think of a situation when you overused this strength and another when you underused it. What were the consequences of each?

Today's Reflection and Writing Prompt

I noticed that the balanced expression of my signature strength was…

Day 7

Review Week 1

I hope this week of exploration helped you develop a more meaningful awareness of your strengths and how they lead to positive outcomes. As a quick review, you:

- Took or re-took the free VIA Survey and explored resources at VIACharacter.org on Day 1.
- Noticed how a signature strength authentically reflects you at your best on Day 2.
- Imagined life without one of your signature strengths on Day 3.
- Explored a character strength that didn't resonate but noticed how it contributed to your life on Day 4.
- Explored a phasic strength on Day 5.
- Applied the lens of balance to a signature strength on Day 6.

Well done! You've covered much ground in a short time. Take a moment to give yourself a high five for your hard work and Perseverance!

Many people don't have such an awareness of their strengths. Now you have a process for expanding that awareness and practice. You can continue to use these activities over and over to explore additional strengths.

If you're interested in a deeper exploration of your strengths, the VIA Institute offers a report called the VIA Pro Report (available for purchase at https://tinyurl.com/VIA-pro-report). This report offers an in-depth look at your signature strengths and insights to help you understand your strengths profile. Some people find it helpful to have this report debriefed by a strengths-based professional. If

Congratulations on your progress!

you're interested, I can help with that. Email me at Jane@ StrengthBasedLiving.com.

We began this week with a quote:

> *"Make the most of yourself…for that is all there is of you."*
>
> —Ralph Waldo Emerson

This quote is a message of Hope. You have a unique profile of strengths. You can engage your strengths often and intentionally to benefit you and other people. That is all there is of you and that is enough.

Today's Activity

1. Is there a strength you want to better understand or feel more confident about? Is there another one that doesn't resonate with you? Is there one you want to boost? Choose a character strength and repeat any of the practices from this week to deepen your awareness of who you are and what you do when at your best.

2. Repeat this process at any time, now or in the future, to continue expanding your understanding of how these character strengths are pathways to success and well-being.

Today's Reflection and Writing Prompt

Intentionally expressing myself at my best feels…

WEEK

2

Connecting & Building Relationships (Strengths-Spotting)

"It's not what you look at that matters. It's what you see."

—Henry David Thoreau

Welcome to Week 2!

When you look at the image below, what do you see? Take a good long look before continuing.

A beautiful young woman, head turned away? Or an old woman in profile? After looking more closely at this image by cartoonist W. E. Hill, entitled *My Wife and My Mother-In-Law,* can you see both?

Regardless of what you first saw, there's often more to the picture. If you take a fresh look or consider a different perspective of this picture, of yourself, of another person, or of the present moment, there's almost always more to see.

The driver who cut you off in traffic might be rushing to a family emergency at the hospital. The short-tempered colleague at work might be worried about losing her job. I'm not condoning bad or hurtful behavior, but there's often more to the picture.

"It's not what you look at that matters. It's what you see."

It matters how you see other people and how you see yourself. It matters because it influences how you feel, how you react, and what action you take or don't take.

The activities in Week 2 help you connect and build positive relationships as you learn to see people, even those you might not care for, through a lens of strengths.

Day 8

Spot strengths in video characters

I recently heard about a young student with learning disabilities being mainstreamed through public school. He was viewed by most of his teachers, as well as classmates and their parents, as disruptive and difficult. The staff and his parents focused mainly on improving his behavior. His behavior improved little over the years.

One astute teacher decided to focus on his strengths, among which were his keen sense of Humor and his active imagination, Creativity. She wondered how he could apply these strengths in the classroom to cultivate engagement and compassion for others.

She asked for his thoughts and worked with his parents to create the conditions in which he could apply his strengths. Together, they found new and productive ways for him to engage. He became a beloved member of the class. He grew up and became a successful artist.

How many teachers, managers, parents, leaders, coaches, and students do you know who cultivate strengths? Hopefully many. If not, you're in good company.

As a society we seem to focus more easily on problems, challenges, and opportunities to improve. The struggling or disruptive student. The complaining customers. Underperforming employees.

There's another view. There is something good in every person, group, and organization. Something that works. Strengths. To cultivate these strengths, you must first notice them all around and within you. The practice of noticing and appreciating strengths is called *strengths-spotting*.

Strengths-spotting is a skill that builds *strengths fluency*, the knowledge, language, and deeper understanding of char-

> To develop a more meaningful awareness of strengths, you must first notice them within yourself and other people.

acter strengths. Developing this fluency prepares us for the more practical step of developing and applying strengths. My colleagues and I find that strengths-spotting also cultivates positive relationships, the number one predictor of happiness.

It's like learning a foreign language that then helps you to connect with people, explore new territory, and thrive in a foreign country. It's a practice you can learn and easily integrate into your daily life.

Many people can intuitively spot strengths in others. It's also a skill that you can develop with practice.

This week is about building your strengths fluency through the foundational practice of strengths-spotting. If there is only one practice you master in these 30 days, it should be this one. When you openly acknowledge and value strengths in action, you're likely to make someone else's day, transform a stressful conversation, or view yourself with compassion in a difficult moment. You're likely to boost feelings of warmth, connection, and admiration as you elevate the good.

You can spot strengths in yourself and others including friends, family, colleagues, and even your favorite book, movie, or TV characters. The process is quite simple:

1. Notice and name the strengths you see in yourself or someone else.

2. Express appreciation for those strengths.

3. Describe how they contributed to the present moment or situation.

Spotting strengths in action takes practice, however. It requires that you slow down, perhaps shift from what's wrong, and use a strengths lens to see what's strong. You can look and listen for signs your strengths are engaged, such as:

1. Energy and excitement

2. A feeling of confidence and mastery

3. A sense of ease

4. Expansiveness in the mind or body

In contrast, when you're not at your best or focusing on a weakness, you might notice:

1. More self-criticism
2. Less confidence
3. Feelings of frustration or impatience
4. Disengagement
5. Narrowing of thinking
6. A sense of unease
7. Appearing closed physically or defensive

Strengths-spotting makes the world a better place. It is almost always a welcome and needed change from what's not going well. As a dear colleague of mine said after we spotted strengths in one another, "This never gets old!"

> Strengths-spotting is a great way to shift into a positive mindset and begin a dialogue about what's going well.

Today's Activity

1. Watch a short, inspirational video of friends playing hockey (at https://tinyurl.com/friends-playing-hockey).

2. List each strength you spot in the two main characters and examples of how they used it. For instance, the friend used Kindness to help his buddy score a goal. He was Loving in the way he helped guide his buddy, and so on.

3. Challenge yourself to spot as many of the 24 strengths as possible.

4. Bonus question: What character strengths did you spot in the goalie and other players in the background?

5. Notice how it feels to appreciate the strengths in other people, even if you don't know them personally.

Today's Reflection and Writing Prompt

Strengths-spotting other people feels like…

Day 9

Spot strengths in yourself

I was recently discussing my own introduction to strengths work with a colleague. We were both participants in an 11-month course called Certificate in Positive Psychology (CiPP) led by Tal Ben-Shahar, Maria Sirois, and Megan McDonough. We were assigned the following "You At Your Best" activity:

> *"Think of a time when you were at your best. It can be something that took place recently, last week, last month, or years ago. You felt engaged or highly connected with what you were doing. You were performing at your best or maybe even stretching beyond what you thought you were capable of.*
>
> *Perhaps you succeeded at accomplishing something meaningful or important to you. Or maybe you were very happy in your life, and you were part of creating that happiness. What strengths contributed to your accomplishment or success?"*

Some of us have difficulty articulating who we are and what we do when at our best. Reflecting on your best moments and observing your strengths in those moments can expand your self-awareness.

According to research, people who write about and reflect on this every day for a week experience more well-being and less depression.[1]

I commented to my friend that when I first read the assignment, I was surprised to find that literally no examples came to mind. I scanned my memory and even looked through old photo albums. Still, nothing. I wasn't accustomed to thinking about myself at my best, although I could imagine an infinite number of difficult times and things that didn't go well.

I remember trying to shift gears, thinking of what I was good at. I was a dedicated, patient parent. I was acknowledged at work for leading successful teams, improving quality, and energizing work environments. I overcame breast cancer. Twice.

Still, I couldn't think of examples that really spoke to the assignment of feeling highly engaged and connected. It's not that I disliked my work or life, but I often felt like the proverbial hamster spinning on the wheel.

It was painful to think that I had lived more than half my life and yet was so out of tune with my strengths. It took a little time and a little practice before I could navigate the negativity bias, develop strengths fluency, and feel comfortable spotting strengths in myself even though I could easily see strengths in others.

On a scale of 1 to 10, how well can you describe your strengths and the benefits they lead to in your relationships, health, or work?

My friend shared that she had a similar experience. Many of us do. Yet when I work with groups and individuals, they agree that learning to value what's best in ourselves and others is worth the investment.

Think about how well you can articulate your strengths. On a scale of 1 to 10, where 1 is having no awareness and 10 is being highly aware, how well do you know yours? Do you appreciate how they elevate who you are and what you do when at your best?

Try spotting strengths in yourself in a best moment. The more you practice, the easier it gets. Take the time to appreciate and celebrate the unique combination of strengths that help you bring forth your best in the world.

Today's Activity

1. Complete the "You At Your Best" exercise offered at the beginning of this day.

2. Be sure to name your strengths and write about how they contributed to your success, strengthened a relationship, created meaning, or led to happiness.

Today's Reflection and Writing Prompt

Spotting strengths I see in myself is...because...

Is it difficult? Easy? Natural? Uncomfortable? Awkward? Something you often do? Something you rarely do? It might be some of these or something else entirely.

Day 10

Notice your strengths in action throughout the day

Although you and I have our own unique profiles of character strengths, we have what experts refer to as *strengths blindness* in common. Strengths blindness is an inability to recognize strengths in ourselves and others, at least some of the time.[2]

Even the most experienced strengths practitioners are occasionally blind to lower and middle strengths. Even the most practiced professionals sometimes dismiss signature strengths as ordinary rather than extraordinary. We operate on autopilot without full awareness of what we focus on, how we feel, what we accomplish and how we impact others. We don't always see the whole picture or the strengths that can help us.

If one of your signature strengths is Social Intelligence, know that not everyone is so intuitive about the impact of words and actions on others. If a signature strength is Leadership, not everyone can rally a team to achieve an important goal the way you can.

You might think you only express your strengths in best or heroic moments. That's not the case. It's likely that you use all 24 character strengths every day. Not only your signature strengths, but all 24. You're already using them in both exciting and mundane, spontaneous and planned, new and routine activities you complete throughout the day.

Don't believe it? Stop right now as you're reading this and ask yourself: What strengths was I just using? I imagine Love of Learning because you're learning about character strengths. Self-regulation as you focus your attention on this practice. Kindness toward yourself for carving out time

> It's likely that you use your character strengths throughout the day, not just in best moments.

to practice. Possibly Gratitude for being part of a positive learning community.

The key to today's activity is leaving the autopilot mind behind and becoming mindful of the strengths you're already using day in and day out. If you find it difficult to see strengths in yourself, if you view the lower strengths as weaknesses, or if you experience autopilot mind frequently, this activity will help you see yourself through a lens of strengths. It will shift your awareness and help you see that there are infinite new ways to engage your strengths in each moment as it unfolds, no matter what you're doing.

Today's Activity*

It might be helpful to have your ranked list of 24 character strengths on hand for this activity. Or use the VIA Classification of Strengths and Virtues, located at the beginning of this book, as an aid.

1. Set an alert periodically throughout your day, perhaps every hour or two, depending on your schedule.

2. When the alert sounds, pause and ask yourself: What strengths was I just using? List each strength and a brief phrase or description of how you used it.

3. How did that strength benefit you or someone else? Did it improve your mood? Boost your confidence? Help you understand someone or a situation more clearly, more compassionately? Accomplish something new? Solve a problem? Write down all the benefits you see from using that strength.

Today's Reflection and Writing Prompt

Spotting my strengths throughout the day helped me see that…

*Based on Character Strength Intervention (CSI) 8 in *Character Strengths Interventions: A Field Guide for Practitioners* by Ryan Niemiec.

Day 11

Make someone else's day through strengths-spotting

When someone else sees the best in us, it feels good to be acknowledged and appreciated.

Recently, I was preparing for a webinar with two colleagues. It was about nine minutes before the starting time. There were numerous technical problems that needed to be re-solved, and tensions were rising.

Our tech support expert, whom I had met only virtually, was unfazed and methodical as she expertly led us through various troubleshooting questions, exuding a calm mas-tery of her duties. It's such a pleasure to work with people like this. They give a sense of comfort and confidence that everything will be fine. In this situation, it was.

Just before we started, I wanted to show my appreciation, so I acknowledged her strengths.

"Ellen (not her real name), your Perspective and Judgment, Perseverance, and Creativity are amazing! I appreciate how instantaneously you analyzed the details, saw the bigger picture, used your Creativity to connect the dots, and effec-tively resolved the issues. Your mastery helped me feel more relaxed and confident that the technology would be stable."

Suddenly it got quiet. After composing herself, Ellen said, "You don't know how much that means to me. It has been a really hard day."

What an unexpected response! I imagine she felt seen and understood. Perhaps relieved or even joyful. The mood lightened, and we spotted strengths in each other for a few additional moments. It was a huge positivity booster. Ac-cording to Peterson and Seligman, merely naming a strength in someone seems to have the benefit of amplifying it.[3]

> Strengths-spotting others can help them feel seen and valued for who they are. It's a practice that can literally transform someone's day.

Later that day she emailed to thank me for that moment. It was a turning point in her day, and she was able to resolve other difficulties more easily and confidently as a result. Another unexpected wave of pure pleasure!

To have someone else name our strengths in action is such a gift. We feel seen and understood for who we really are. It can start a ripple effect of positive emotions that can deepen a relationship. Shift tension in the moment. Change the trajectory of a day. It's not an exaggeration to say that many moments of strengths-spotting are transformational.

We aren't often able to see the ripple effects of our actions, but in this case, I experienced it firsthand. The lesson? It's what you see that matters.

Do you want to make someone else's day? Shift a negative internal dialogue? Connect more deeply with a colleague? Acknowledge his or her strengths. Even if you don't get to experience the ripple effect, know that it's there.

Today's Activity

1. Choose someone you know well or an acquaintance at work or home. Don't choose someone with whom you have a difficult relationship. Save that for later.

2. Write down the top 3 to 5 character strengths you see in that person, and an example of how he/she used each strength.

3. Share your thoughts with him or her. Face-to-face is usually best, but a phone call, email, or letter also works.

Today's Reflection and Writing Prompt

Strengths-spotting with my friend/colleague/acquaintance influenced our relationship because…

Day 12

Boost the effectiveness of your strengths-spotting

Hopefully by now you've experienced positive outcomes from the foundational practice of strengths-spotting. In my experience, you can boost the potency of your strengths-spotting even more.

If you and I worked on the same team, and I said to you after a meeting with the boss, "I noticed your Bravery in action today," how might you respond?

It's nice to be noticed, right? I named the strength and shared it with you. Sometimes, however, the person on the receiving end doesn't respond well because the experience lacks context. There's no connection between his actions and a positive outcome.

Adding details, context, and value is where the gold is. What if I said this instead, "When you stood up to our boss and put a stake in the ground for our team, the whole conversation shifted. I appreciated the Bravery it took and your professionalism in representing us so well."

It's more specific. I provided context and details, referring to what you were doing while engaging your strength of Bravery. I expressed the impact it had on me and the team.

I'd like to offer another example: "Dad, when you fixed my dripping faucet, I felt supported and well cared for. I think that's your Love and Kindness coming through. Thank you."

Ryan Niemiec says the potency of strengths-spotting increases when naming and discussing the rationale and value spontaneously.[4]

> Acknowledging peoples' strengths in action, providing specific examples, and expressing your appreciation can boost the potency of your strengths-spotting.

Overwhelmingly, people I work with find it easier to re-flect on past examples of strengths use rather than catch-ing examples of strengths in action as they unfold. That's why today's activity is about boosting the potency of your strengths-spotting as you practice the following steps:

1. Name a strength in action as you notice it.

2. Provide the context with examples and details of when and how the person used that strength.

3. Express why you valued or appreciated it.

You may feel awkward at first, but your strengths-spotting will flow more naturally as you practice.

Today's Activity

1. Look for a situation in which things are going well. This is a prime opportunity to spot the strengths in someone else. Look and listen for the signs of strengths in action.

2. Practice strengths-spotting in the moment, following the three steps.

3. Notice how it feels, how he or she responds, and what happens next.

Today's Reflection and Writing Prompt

Strengths-spotting with intention was…

Day 13

Spot strengths in someone you don't care for

Although I try to see the best in others, I sometimes meet people who just rub me the wrong way. I imagine you know people like this, too. The brash family member who insults everyone at family events. The co-worker who acts like a know-it-all but doesn't back it up. The overly vocal skeptic in the audience at your last presentation. I'm not talking about psychopaths, just people I don't mesh with.

A basic premise of positive psychology is that within *each* person, even the annoying one, there is goodness and potential. Can you envision what might happen if we could see this person through a lens of strengths?

Applying a lens of strengths to someone who rubs you the wrong way can dramatically change your perspective.

A participant in a group was discussing a difficult family member, her husband. Of course she loved him, but she thought he was being dismissive in their shared Leadership of the family business.

I listened while she recounted the many grievances she had. She was clearly at her wit's end and had no idea how to improve the situation.

I sensed it was a good time to shift the conversation to strengths. We got into a lengthy conversation about what was going well, and the strengths she saw and appreciated in her husband. She saw Kindness, Love, and Social Intelligence. She gave examples of how his strengths helped build trusting relationships with their clients.

She noted his Love of Learning and Curiosity, which he used to stay on top of industry trends. He engaged Judgment and Prudence to integrate trends into their business strategy. Their business was thriving even though their relationship wasn't.

As she spoke, it became clear that using a strengths lens was shifting her perspective of her husband from a difficult person to someone she admired. She realized that his strengths were, in part, what she found attractive in him when they first met.

She began thinking of these signature strengths as gifts to the business and their life together. Rather than seeing him as distant, she noticed his underuse of Love, Kindness, and Social Intelligence toward her because they had been so busy growing the business.

> When you see people with whom you don't get along through a lens of strengths, you might discover something new or rediscover who they are when at their best.

She also noted her own underuse of Honesty about the toll it was taking on her and her overuse of Perseverance on projects that didn't align with his priorities.

In those moments, she transformed physically and emotionally. Her face shifted from frowning to softly smiling. Her language shifted from harsh to positive. Her body relaxed. Becoming more thoughtful and open, she was getting herself unstuck and beginning to solve problems in a new way.

We discussed how they could have a strengths-based conversation, and they did. They named and appreciated each other's strengths. They were able to move through this difficulty and collaborate on their business and personal relationship again.

She reported that this exercise helped her see what works in her husband and use *that* as a starting point for discussion rather than her complaints and grievances.

Using a strengths lens isn't a magic bullet for every person and situation, but we can certainly use this approach more often. When confronted by an aggressive heckler in the audience during a presentation, a mentor of mine spotted the heckler's obvious Love of Learning, and Judgment, albeit perhaps overused. She invited him to find a case study to back up his claims and offered to share it with the other participants. This was strength-based problem solving in action.

If you could look at someone you don't care for through a lens of strengths, what and who might you see? From there, what might be possible? Even if you decide not to share what you see, how might *you* change in that moment?

Today's Activity

1. Think of someone you don't care for or an interaction that rubbed you the wrong way. Don't choose someone who is toxic to your relationship or has hurt you deeply in the past.

2. Notice your thoughts and what you feel in your body as you think about this person.

3. Identify 3-5 signature strengths you spot in this person and examples of how he/she engages them.

4. In this interaction, notice if you or this person overused or underused strengths. Refer to Day 6 if you'd like a refresher on strengths overuse and underuse.

5. Notice any changes in your body, thoughts, or feelings.

6. If you feel comfortable, share the strengths you spotted with this person. Don't forget to add context and why you value those strengths.

Today's Reflection and Writing Prompt

Applying strengths-spotting to someone I don't care for shifted...

Day 14

Review Week 2 and integrate a strengths-spotting activity

This week you practiced the skill of strengths-spotting. As a quick review, you:

- Spotted strengths in young hockey players and perhaps noticed how intuitive strengths-spotting can be on Day 8.
- Reminded yourself of who you are at your best by spotting strengths in yourself on Day 9.
- Monitored your activities throughout the day and noticed how often you engaged your character strengths on Day 10.
- Made someone else's day on Day 11 by spotting strengths in him or her in the moment.
- Boosted the potency of your strengths-spotting on Day 12.
- Viewed someone you don't care for through a lens of strengths on Day 13 and perhaps noticed a positive shift within yourself, the situation, and your relationship.

Well done! Take a moment to give yourself a well-deserved high five!

Although strengths-spotting is a simple and foundational practice, many of us haven't integrated the practice enough to experience the benefits. Below are a few simple practices my clients rave about because they are both easy and effective.

1. Spot strengths in yourself before tackling a stressful activity, for example, an important meeting you're

My clients comment that they feel confident and motivated to finish important goals when intentionally using their strengths. Remember to keep using yours to stay engaged.

68

about to lead, a difficult conversation you need to have, or any task that stretches you beyond your comfort zone.

2. At family dinner time, take turns spotting strengths in each family member. Make sure everyone has an opportunity to have their strengths spotted.

3. Begin a team meeting at work with what went well, spot the strengths in each team member, and mention how they contributed to success. If you're interested in exploring how to amplify strengths on your team, email me at Jane@StrengthBasedLiving.com. Also, the VIA Institute on Character offers a VIA Pro Team Report (available at https://tinyurl.com/VIA-Team-Report) and a course called Developing Effective Teams (available at https://tinyurl.com/Developing-Effective-Teams).

4. Send a daily strengths-spotting email to colleagues, friends, family, or anyone whose strengths you'd like to recognize.

A regular strengths-spotting practice will connect you more deeply with others and give a nice boost to these important relationships.

Today's Activity

1. Choose one of the strengths-spotting practices and integrate it into your day.

2. Try it for a week. Do it concurrently with Week 3 or begin Week 3 after your strengths-spotting practice takes hold. Feel free to choose based on your schedule and interests.

Today's Reflection and Writing Prompt

Looking for strengths helps shift my perspective on…

WEEK

3

Boosting Your Confidence & Competence (Developing Strengths)

> *"At any moment, you have a choice that either leads you closer to your spirit or further away from it."*
>
> —Thich Nhat Hanh

Welcome to Week 3!

We make choices every day. What to eat for breakfast. How much time to spend with friends or loved ones. When to ask for more responsibility at work. These choices either elevate us in some way by boosting health, a relationship, our own sense of self, or they don't.

Investing in strengths is also a choice. Research consistently shows that building strengths is more effective than focusing on weaknesses. Positive psychology expert Robert Biswas-Diener says that:

> *"...energy invested in strengths will lead to a disproportionately large gain relative to a comparable investment in weaknesses."*[1]

Developing strengths requires identifying and engaging them frequently, which you practiced in Weeks 1 and 2.

There are many resources available to support you. You've already seen some of them on the VIA website.

You might also consult the long list of activities, songs, and movies for building character strengths collected by Tayyab Rashid and Afroze Anjum (available at https://tinyurl. com/BuildVIAStrengths). Or pick up a copy of *Character Strengths Matter: How to Live a Full Life* (available at https:// tinyurl.com/CharStrengthsMatter). This approachable book shares stories from positive psychology experts along with activities that engage each character strength.

This week, you'll acquire a more nuanced understanding of how to use your strengths *well* and how to navigate their shadow side. As you develop your strengths, notice how they define the essence of you.

Day 15

Apply the Golden Mean of strengths

Until now, we've focused on one character strength at a time. This approach is intentional because it is simpler to start without worrying about how character strengths interact with each other.

In daily life, though, we rarely engage one strength at a time. Instead, we use combinations of character strengths. Love and Kindness are a common combination, as are Curiosity and Love of Learning. Strengths working together are typically referred to as *strengths constellations*.

The way you express combinations of strengths is unique to you. Suppose you and your best friend are both high in Appreciation of Beauty and Excellence, and you decide to enjoy a sunset together. If Curiosity is also your friend's top strength and Love is yours, you're likely to have different experiences of the sunset.

She might wonder what lies beyond the horizon, or how the explorers felt when discovering land. You might have thoughts about a loved one and when the two of you will see the sunset together again.

To make things even more complex, you must draw on different combinations of strengths to navigate situations you encounter each day. If a friend is ill and wants your company, he might need your Love and Kindness but probably not your Judgment and Love of Learning…until he asks you to research the types of medical help available. Then, your Judgment and Love of Learning might be more helpful.

The context matters a lot, and it changes often. We can learn to apply the right combinations to the right degree based

Excellence often comes from multiple strengths working together.

on what the situation calls for. Experts refer to this as the *optimal level of strengths expression*, or the *Golden Mean*. The Golden Mean is:

> *"...the right combination of strengths, used to the right degree, in the right situation for a purpose that benefits both self and others."*[2]

For instance, a client was preparing for a work call with someone who had stepped on her toes the previous week. She practiced Forgiveness toward this person, Kindness toward herself, and Prudence to plan the call. She engaged the Golden Mean. As a result, she felt confident, conducted herself professionally, and accomplished her goals for the call.

Too much Forgiveness or Kindness would have left her feeling like a doormat, diminishing her confidence. Too much Prudence would have resulted in being overly cautious, too guarded for the situation. Too little and her emotions could have governed the conversation. Engaging strengths in an unbalanced way typically leads to negative outcomes.

Seeking the Golden Mean is a way to think differently about your interactions throughout the day. Part art and part science, it doesn't come with an instruction manual, but you can become more practiced at it.

Give it a go. When you finish today's practice, what task comes next? Will you prepare for a call at work? Make lunch? Do something else?

Seeking the Golden Mean, the optimal expression of strengths, helps you avoid unintended negative consequences of underusing and overusing your strengths.

74

Today's Activity

1. Identify the task that comes next in your day.

2. What combination of strengths will you need to complete this task? Identify at least two, preferably three or more. To what degree?

3. Envision what too much or too little of these strengths might look and feel like, and what the outcomes might be. Feel free to use the Character Strengths Overuse and Underuse table, located at the back of the book, as a resource.

4. Now that you are prepared to use the Golden Mean of your strengths, complete the task in your day.

Today's Reflection & Writing Prompt

When I engaged the Golden Mean of my strengths, something that went well was…

Day 16

Temper an overused strength

My partner and I are currently renovating our house. We've reconfigured rooms, replaced windows, removed wallpaper, installed new molding, and taken on many other projects ourselves without hiring professionals.

When I say "ourselves," I mean my partner. I dream it, and he builds it. It's a lot of work, and although I'm available to help, he dedicates many more labor hours to the cause.

Recently, he was attempting to attach a finishing piece to the bottom of the kitchen cabinets. I saw him wrestling with it and figured he could use a little Humor break. I launched into my favorite "knock knock" joke.

"Hey, knock knock," I started and waited for the standard reply "Who's there?" No reply. So I tried a second time, a bit louder.

"Knock knock."

No reply again. I drew closer, thinking maybe he didn't hear me, but he turned and looked at me with that look. You know, the one that without a word being spoken says, "Don't bother me right now, I'm in the middle of something."

I noticed that he was struggling with the materials to get the fit right, muscling them into place, and not having a good time doing it. I became acutely aware of my overuse of Humor and underuse of Social Intelligence.

Not only did he not need a Humor break at this time, but if I had put myself in his shoes I would have noticed that his frustration level was growing. My approach was making things worse. Not exactly a relationship booster!

Overusing a strength can unintentionally strain a relationship and become a source of conflict or stress.

76

While this example of Humor overuse wouldn't destroy our relationship, imagine over time if I were this insensitive to my partner if he was suffering from an illness or dealing with a family emergency. If I worked with clients in this way, I wouldn't be very busy.

Research shows that the optimal use of strengths is linked with significantly higher flourishing, higher life satisfaction, and less depression. Overuse and underuse are linked with *less* flourishing, *less* life satisfaction, and *higher* depression.[3]

It's especially easy to overuse signature strengths without noticing because we express them so naturally. However, we can overuse any of the 24 character strengths, often to the detriment of ourselves and our relationships. Ryan Niemiec notes that:

> *"Often, strengths overuse has an impact on relationships and the individual who is doing the overusing is unaware (i.e., blind) to this impact or at least the extent of the impact."*[4]

Once you become aware of overusing a strength, you can rein it in or engage a more helpful strength.

You're probably familiar with the know-it-all overusing Love of Learning. Or the person without a filter overusing Honesty. Or the nosy person overusing Curiosity. Perhaps *you* have been that person from time to time.

This overuse can block your attempts to connect with others. By looking at each situation through a lens of strengths, you will discover a new framework for managing relationship issues. Within this framework are two key strategies:

- Temper the overused strength. Bring it down a notch.
- Elevate a different, more helpful strength.

In the situation with my partner, I could have put a pause on Humor and instead used Curiosity, one of my signature strengths, to ask: "How's it going? Is now a good time for a quick Humor break? Is there anything I can do to help?" This would have been much more appropriate given the situation. He could have explained that it wasn't a good time, and I would have understood.

Today's practice is about noticing when you tend to overuse strengths and which of your other strengths would help temper or balance that overuse.

Today's Activity*

1. As you go about your day today, notice a strength you overuse.

2. Next, notice how this overuse impacts you, a relationship, and the situation.

3. Identify other strengths that balance the overuse and notice how they will be helpful.

4. Engage these other strengths to temper the overuse.

Today's Reflection and Writing Prompt

What I learned from tempering an overused strength was...

*Adapted from Character Strength Intervention (CSI) 58 in *Character Strengths Interventions: A Field Guide for Practitioners* by Ryan Niemiec.

Day 17

Amplify an underused strength

Recently I was helping a colleague review the results of his strengths survey. He became curious about his middle strength, Creativity, and wanted to talk about using it more often. When I asked why, he replied that his coaching sessions seemed stale, and he wondered whether Creativity could help. He didn't view himself as a particularly Creative person, but he was up for the challenge.

We brainstormed ways he could boost Creativity in his coaching sessions. We created new questions he could ask clients, a game he could introduce, and changes that might improve the flow of the session.

He tried these ideas with clients he thought would be receptive. Notice his use of Social Intelligence here. He realized that applying Creativity in different ways enlivened him and his clients. The sessions felt more fun and productive. His clients loved it and gave him glowing reviews.

> Boosting an underused strength can enliven you, your work, and your relationships. It is one of the most effective ways to benefit from your strengths.

To determine which of your strengths can help you more, ask yourself three questions:

1. Which strengths do I tend to underuse?
2. Which strengths do I need more of *right now?*
3. Which other strengths might help me use this strength more?

Depending on the context, you might see opportunities to elevate a signature, middle, or lower strength. For instance, when working towards a deadline on a project I don't enjoy, I tend to underuse Zest, a middle strength. Wanting to finish, I push myself for hours even as I become tired, cranky, and less productive. Taking periodic exercise breaks boosts my Zest and helps me regain energy and enthusiasm so I can continue without pushing myself over the edge. It doesn't change the subject or the deadline, but it changes me.

When I'm faced with serious life matters such as a loss or an illness, I notice far less Humor within and around me. Without enough Humor, life seems empty. I feel depleted. When I intentionally engage Humor at appropriate times, I feel enlivened. My perspective shifts in a positive direction, even if momentarily.

Whether you're working on something new at work or caring for a sick relative, you're likely to have underused strengths that will support you by boosting your confidence, energy, resilience, and performance.

Today's Activity*

1. Begin by noticing a strength you tend to underuse or ask yourself which strength can help you *right now*.

2. Identify at least one way to use this strength in your personal or professional life, within a relationship, or to boost your health or resilience. Then try it out.

Today's Reflection and Writing Prompt

When I elevated an underused strength, I was able to…

*Based on Character Strength Intervention (CSI) 19 in *Character Strengths Interventions: A Field Guide for Practitioners* by Ryan Niemiec.

Day 18

Manage colliding strengths

There are literally hundreds of research-based reasons to engage one's strengths. Some relate to the workplace, education, disability, life satisfaction, and health and wellness. Others relate to achievement, mental illness, mindfulness, relationships, special populations, and other arenas.

Unfortunately, there are also potential downsides to engaging one's strengths. These downsides aren't often discussed, but you need to know that your strengths are not a cure-all. Using your strengths doesn't come with a guarantee that you will experience desired outcomes.

For instance, not everyone feels the way you do about your highest strengths, and you won't necessarily value other peoples' highest strengths if they're different from yours. Consider the following remark by Robert Biswas-Diener and colleagues:

> *"...because strengths are closely aligned with values (Peterson & Seligman, 2004), it is possible that people will not value the strengths of others if they are different from their own... Someone low in forgiveness, for example, may interpret forgiving behaviors as a sign of weakness in others."* [5]

If you're high in Forgiveness and your boss is low, she might perceive your Forgiveness as a weakness, even as you naturally engage it as a strength.

Someone low in Prudence might view a Prudent person as unwilling to take a risk rather than being careful. Those low in Creativity might view Creative people as flaky. Those low in Self-regulation might view someone higher in Self-regulation as inflexible. Some people value Fairness, Honesty, or Kindness more than others. You could select any of the

You can learn to navigate moments when your attempts to engage strengths go unnoticed or aren't appreciated by others.

24 character strengths and see how others respond to them differently, depending on what their profiles look like.

Another downside is that your strengths can collide with other people's strengths. Imagine that a teammate's signature strength is Creativity and yours is Judgment. In a perfect world, the team would capitalize on his Creativity by asking him to lead a brainstorming session. The team would also capitalize on your Judgment by asking you to analyze potential solutions.

What might happen if you, with your Judgment, dismiss ideas before the brainstorming session ends? Conflict. What might happen if the Creative person introduces more possibilities when you're analyzing the best options? More conflict.

Other strengths can collide, such as a colleague's Humility and your Bravery. A colleague's Humility and your Bravery. These collisions cause conflict and stress, frustration and anger. It can feel painful to be at odds with someone important in your life and not understand why.

Fortunately, you can learn to identify these collisions. The next time you notice a knot in your stomach, a racing heart, or a sense of frustration, look at the strengths in play. Then respond from a position of strength rather than from frustration or anger.

Today's Activity

1. Think of a situation in your personal or professional life when your strengths collided with someone else's strengths.

2. What strengths did you use? What strengths did the other person use?

3. How could understanding the collision have helped you handle the situation differently?

Today's Reflection and Writing Prompt

Although my strengths are not a cure-all, I can access them at any time to…

Day 19

Engage the "achievement strength"

In her book, *Getting Grit: The Evidence-Based Approach to Cultivating Passion, Perseverance, and Purpose,* positive psychology expert and bestselling author Caroline Miller shines a light on the challenge of achieving hard goals. She says that people who achieve hard goals not only work hard, but also overcome difficulties without losing focus, equanimity, or passion.

It's not only about being focused and putting in the time, though. She goes on to say that if you "…don't have a constructive relationship with discomfort, failure, and delayed gratification, it's imperative to find ways to make your peace with these conditions."[6] This comes from a chapter devoted to Perseverance.

> Perseverance regularly shows up in studies about achievement.

The character strength Perseverance shows up regularly in studies about achievement. From your survey results, notice that Perseverance is defined as: finishing what one starts; persevering in a course of action in spite of obstacles; getting it out the door; taking pleasure in completing tasks.

Consider the following findings about Perseverance in the classroom:

- In a study of middle school and college students, Perseverance, Love, Gratitude, and Hope predicted academic achievement.[7]

- In a study of primary and secondary school students, Perseverance, Social Intelligence, Prudence, Hope, and Self-regulation were associated with positive classroom behavior. In this same study, Perseverance, Love of Learning, Zest, Perspective, Gratitude, and Hope were associated with school achievement.[8]

Consider these findings in the workplace:

- In a workplace study of almost 700 participants, Perseverance was the strength most associated with work productivity and least associated with counter-productive work behaviors.[9]
- Work demands require individuals to use more Perseverance, Love of Learning, Leadership, Curiosity, Self-Control and Prudence than what is natural for them.[10]

When elevated to the right degree, your capacity to Persevere can help you overcome obstacles and achieve hard goals.

One can't help but notice that Perseverance is a common thread. You might wonder whether cultivating a specific strength like Perseverance, and not just signature strengths, is beneficial to achievement.

From a strengths development perspective, the question is which strategy boosts achievement more effectively: engaging a specific strength like Perseverance or engaging one's signature strengths?

It seems that both strategies yield positive outcomes when used in the right amount. Whether Perseverance is a signature, middle, or lower strength, you can view this strength as a pathway to achievement.

The young adult who dropped out of college to launch a successful new business Persevered with one goal, even though he abandoned another. The newlyweds who did what was necessary to pay off their student loans Persevered. They had hard goals and probably overcame obstacles to achieve them.

There is so much more to know about setting and achieving goals, but today's activity is about reaching for a goal using Perseverance, the achievement strength. Use it to keep going and maybe even finish what you started.

Today's Activity

1. Choose an important or hard goal that you're currently working toward. What steps will you take to finish what you started?

2. Write down potential obstacles to achieving this goal. How do you typically respond to these obstacles?

3. If you feel discomfort or fear of failure, which of your strengths will help you?

4. As you work on your goal, remember your capacity to Persevere and to engage other strengths that will help you achieve it.

Today's Reflection and Writing Prompt

When I feel like giving up on an important goal, I Persevere by...

Day 20

Practice a "happiness strength"

One of the most unifying goals in humanity is a desire to be happy. We wish happiness for our children, families, friends, and ourselves. It's in our nature to pursue happiness. The pursuit of happiness is even one of three unalienable rights in the United States Declaration of Independence.

Understanding what boosts happiness is another matter. Many of us believe that happiness is a destination, an endpoint after achieving an important goal.

Take a moment to think of the important goals you've achieved. Perhaps you aced an exam, got a promotion, or decided to retire. You probably spent hours, weeks, or years preparing and then celebrating your accomplishment, but how long did that boost your happiness? A few days? A few hours?

It seems we're not very good at predicting what will make us happy in the long run. The benefits of worthy goals are undeniable, but a higher grade point average, more disposable income, and a flexible schedule don't directly create lasting happiness. We need worthy goals *and* an ability to enjoy the journey toward those goals.

Your character strengths can help you enjoy that journey. In a *Psychology Today* article, Niemiec names Gratitude, Hope, Zest, Love, and Curiosity as "happiness strengths." From the same article, VIA's research shows that more than three-fourths of us have one of the five happiness strengths in our own top five.[11]

If they're not in *your* top 5, however, you can still use them to cultivate happiness. Following are a few research-based reasons why and how to engage them.

Gratitude, Hope, Zest, Love, and Curiosity are known as "happiness strengths." Engage them to enjoy your journey toward a worthy goal like finishing this 30-day practice.

Gratitude

Individuals high in Gratitude constantly notice and appreciate the blessings in their lives. Grateful people typically don't take things and people for granted or feel a sense of entitlement.

Dr. Robert Emmons, a leading expert in the science of gratitude, says that gratitude is one of the few things that can measurably change peoples' lives for the better through lower blood pressure, higher immune function, more efficient sleep, lower depression and anxiety, and more resiliency.[12]

In his lectures, Tal Ben-Shahar says that when we appreciate the good, the good appreciates. Studies show that gratitude boosts relationships and motivates employees to work harder in addition to increasing well-being.[13]

A simple way to cultivate Gratitude is to write down three things you're grateful for at the end of each day.[14] To challenge yourself, think of the blessings you might be taking for granted: your spouse who takes the garbage out night after night, your child who put his backpack away after school today, your boss who supported your perspective in a client meeting. Be sure to thank them for enhancing your life, even in a small way.

Hope

Have you heard the phrase "wet blanket" to describe someone who constantly sees all the reasons *not* to try something new or argues why a solution *won't* work? This person is probably underusing Hope.

Those high in Hope tend to: " …look on the bright side of life. They find positives when others see only negatives, and they expect the best for the future. The strength of hope involves believing you can accomplish the goals that you set, even looking bravely beyond obstacles that may arise.

The happiness strengths are shown to cultivate numerous surprising outcomes. Gratitude can help lower your blood pressure and motivate people to work harder. Hope can cultivate resiliency.

Hopeful people tend to be healthier, happier, more resilient, and better able to establish positive and healthy relationships."[15]

See if you can boost your Hope by envisioning yourself achieving a realistic goal. Notice the steps you took to get there. Think about alternative pathways to your goal if the most obvious one gets blocked. Remember past achievements to boost your confidence that you can reach your goal.

Zest

Zest can enliven you when you feel depleted. Love can connect you with others on a deeper level, even in the workplace. Curiosity can lead you to new adventures.

Did you ever see an active 4-year-old and wish you could bottle his energy? That's Zest. Undoubtedly, you express Zest differently than a 4-year-old does.

> *"Zest is a positive trait reflecting a person's approach to life with anticipation, energy, and excitement."*[16]

In a study of over 9,800 employed adults, Zest influenced life satisfaction *and* work satisfaction. Providing that rush of energy, Zest is about getting active and bringing enthusiasm, passion and vitality into your relationships, projects, and life.

Zest is the flip side of burnout. If you're feeling depleted, think about the activities that provide a boost. A simple way to boost your energy and vitality is to exercise. Choose a fun activity with a friend and get a double dose of happiness. If you like roller derby, sledding, walking in nature . . . go for it!

To challenge yourself, take action on a task or goal you'd rather avoid. Set a timer for five minutes and dive in with Zest. You may even find yourself completing the task.

Love

People high in Love naturally connect, build relationships, and care for others. They are open to the love that other people give them. They are warm and caring with the people around them.

Unfortunately, many of us are uncomfortable talking about Love, especially in a professional setting. Teenagers, colleagues, and friends with Love as a top strength often feel disappointed until they realize that cultivating relationships is essential to who they are and how they navigate life.

Try boosting Love by doing a favorite activity with your friend, loved one, or associate. To challenge yourself, get to know people outside of your home. Notice what is important to them. When others demonstrate their Love for you, be open to receiving it.

Happiness is often just one character strength away.

Curiosity

Those high in Curiosity tend to love exploration and adventure. Genuinely interested in people and subjects, they ask lots of questions and pursue novelty.

To boost your Curiosity, try a new restaurant or follow a different path on your daily walk. To challenge yourself, think of a least favorite activity. As you complete that activity, think of two new aspects you hadn't noticed previously. For instance, while doing dishes notice how it provides a short break in your day or that the soap bubbles feel tingly on your skin.

These are just a few ways to cultivate the happiness strengths. As you go forward, remember that greater happiness is often just one character strength away.

Today's Activity

1. Try out one of the activities mentioned to boost your happiness.

2. For additional ideas:

   - Write a Gratitude Letter (see https://ggia.berkeley.edu/practice/gratitude_letter).

   - Complete the Best Possible Self exercise found at https://tinyurl.com/Best-Possible-Self to boost Hope.

   - Watch the delightfully Zesty video "Where the Hell is Matt?" (at http://www.viacharacter.org/www/Character-Strengths/Zest)

   - Listen to your favorite Love song.

   - Be Curious and read about a place you'd like to explore.

Today's Reflection and Writing Prompt

Cultivating a happiness strength resulted in…

Day 21

Review Week 3

This week's activities focused on developing your strengths knowledge and practice. Going deeper like this instills the confidence and competence you need to expand your capabilities and help others do the same.

As a quick review, in Week 3 you:

- Applied the Golden Mean of a strength on Day 15.
- Tempered an overused strength on Day 16.
- Amplified an underused strength on Day 17.
- Managed colliding strengths on Day 18.
- Persevered toward a meaningful goal on Day 19.
- Cultivated a happiness strength on Day 20.

Well done! Give yourself a high five for completing another week! Your confidence and competence will continue to grow each time you practice these activities with different strengths and contexts.

We began this week with a quotation from Thich Nhat Hanh:

> *"At any moment, you have a choice that either leads you closer to your spirit or further away from it."*

Which activities from Week 3 led you closest to your spirit? Perhaps you were drawn to tempering an overused signature strength with a loved one. Today, you'll repeat an activity from Week 3.

You Persevered through the completion of Week 3. Congratulations on this great accomplishment!

Today's Activity

1. Review this week's activities.
2. Choose one activity you'd like to repeat and give it a go.

Today's Reflection and Writing Prompt

I shifted toward my most authentic and best self when...

WEEK

4

Living Your Strengths (Doing More of What You Do Best)

"Breathing in, I see my strengths.

Breathing out, I value my strengths.

Dwelling now in my strengths,

I express myself fully."

—Strengths Gatha written by Ryan Niemiec

Welcome to Week 4!

This week's quotation is a *gatha*, a short verse, poem, or meditation, that brings awareness into our daily lives so that we can focus on things we might take for granted. Like strengths.

Thich Nhat Hanh, spiritual leader and Buddhist monk known for his powerful teachings on mindfulness and peace, says the following about gathas:

> *"When we focus our mind on a gatha, we return to ourselves and become more aware of each action. When the gatha ends, we continue our activity with heightened awareness."*

Niemiec's *strengths* gatha brings focus to strengths. In his gatha, the word "dwelling" always jumps out at me. A dwelling, as a noun, is a shelter or home to live in. Dwelling, as a verb, means living in.

The metaphor of strengths as a home is a good one. A home provides comfort and protection. It's a place to receive nourishment. A place to learn and grow.

"Dwelling now in my strengths, I express myself fully."

Think of it as a place where you can always return. A place where you can refuel and enliven yourself. A place where you can practice living your strengths.

In week 4, you'll practice living your strengths and doing more of what you do best. Notice how this week's activities help you steep yourself in strengths and express yourself fully as you shift into new possibilities.

Day 22

Use the Mindful Pause

A colleague and I were planning to have lunch recently. She called apologetically and asked if we could reschedule. She was preparing for an important presentation the following day, and she felt stressed and pressed for time. Of course, I understood.

"Anything I can do to help?" I asked.

After a brief pause, she replied laughing, "Yes. It would be great if you could write this presentation for me! Or in lieu of that, can you give me a magical tool that will help me feel prepared and confident?"

I *could* think of a tool that might help. It's not magical, but it is one of the briefest and most popular research-based activities I've used myself and taught others. It's called the Mindful Pause.

Mindfulness is an ancient practice rooted in Buddhist teachings from more than 2,500 years ago. The amount of research on mindfulness has grown exponentially. Studies show that mindfulness improves physical and mental health, lowers stress and anxiety, and provides many other benefits.

In a word, mindfulness is awareness. Its opposite is mindlessness, also referred to as autopilot mind. We've all experienced autopilot mind. If you've ever driven a car and suddenly noticed being further down the road without remembering how you got there, your autopilot mind was in action.

The Mindful Pause helps you:

1. short-circuit worry, stress, and autopilot thinking,
2. take advantage of present moment awareness,

> Taking a Mindful Pause can help you shift into your strengths.

95

3. activate character strengths in the moment, and

4. shift your mindset to mindfulness and character strengths.[1]

My colleague quickly learned the Mindful Pause. The simple 2-step process for taking a Mindful Pause is:

1. Pause and take 8-10 deep breaths. Feel each inhalation and exhalation. Focus your mind entirely on the steady rhythm of your breathing.

2. At the end of 8-10 breaths, conclude with a question: Which of my character strengths will I bring forth next?

> You can use the Mindful Pause at any time. It is especially useful during stressful times and when you're transitioning between settings, like from home to school or work to home.

Within 5 minutes, she had practiced it several times and was excited to give it a go.

Fast forward to the day after her presentation. She couldn't wait to share the impact of the Mindful Pause with me.

"I used it before sitting down to work on my presentation. It helped me put a pause on my anxious thoughts about presenting. I was able to reset myself and thus approach the preparation with a sense of excitement rather than fear.

"The strength that came up was Love of Learning, a signature strength. I love to research new topics, and I came across key data that boosted my presentation content tremendously. Plus, while preparing I felt energized and engaged, which was quite a new experience."

Elevating her signature strength, Love of Learning, ignited her confidence and enhanced her presentation with stronger research. In this way, the Mindful Pause was a gateway to new possibilities.

My colleague also used the Mindful Pause as part of her pre-presentation ritual. Her lower strength, Spirituality, came up. She wasn't immediately clear on the connection between Spirituality and her presentation.

As she thought about her own Spirituality, however, a sense of peace came over her. She realized how meaningful her topic was and why she was excited to share it with others. Feeling fueled by Spirituality connected her to meaning and purpose.

Everyone has time to learn and practice the Mindful Pause. Note, though, that it's not about choosing a strength you think you need or want. Instead, it's about letting one emerge into your awareness.

When I take a Mindful Pause, I envision a roulette wheel and notice which character strength the ball lands on when the wheel stops. I use it frequently throughout the day, especially before difficult or stressful conversations and activities. Others use it during moments of transition, like going from work to home or home to school.

With the Mindful Pause, every moment throughout the day is an opportunity for you to feel fueled by strengths and express typically unexpressed parts of yourself.

Today's Activity*

1. Practice the Mindful Pause. Use it as you go about your day to reset yourself and become fueled by strengths. If it's helpful, set an alert as a reminder to practice.

2. Notice when you used the Mindful Pause. Was it during times of stress? Transition? Excitement? Perhaps something else?

Today's Reflection and Writing Prompt

The Mindful Pause opened the door to possibility when…

---

*Based on Character Strength Intervention (CSI) 65 in *Character Strengths Interventions: A Field Guide for Practitioners* by Ryan Niemiec.

Day 23

Turn strengths inward

Have you ever made a mistake, criticized yourself harshly, or pushed yourself fiercely, expecting to be your best under challenging circumstances? We can all answer "yes" to at least one of those questions and probably all of them.

I recently participated in a project team call. It was a monthly status meeting to connect, discuss what was going well, troubleshoot problems, and collaborate on next steps.

A team member had been navigating various difficult life events: the death of a close family member, the illness of another, and the sudden turn of her beloved pet's health.

Through all of this, she modeled how to be resilient and garner meaning from these events, inspiring us along the way. She embodied strength-based living by elevating her strengths even during the most difficult situations.

On the day of the call, her day was just too full. She had too many balls in the air and too few internal reserves to manage everything at once. The call took place during the lunch hour, and her window to get something to eat was closing. There was a noticeable decline in her mood and energy.

We all face choices throughout the day, and at this moment hers were to 1) remain on the call, feeling out of sorts and depleted or 2) leave without completing our team business, knowing she would feel recharged afterwards but also uncomfortable about leaving loose ends.

Turning character strengths inward, she realized how hungry she was (Honesty), decided to excuse herself (Kindness), and accepted her need to nourish her body (Forgiveness). Once nourished and refreshed, she could continue being her best.

> Turning your strengths inward can help you treat yourself with compassion, as you would a dear friend.

98

Brilliant! The whole team appreciated her use of Honesty, Kindness, and Forgiveness as she applied them to herself in that moment. She gave herself permission to recharge. We were happy to tie up the loose ends after she excused herself. As a team we felt more deeply connected because we had each other's backs.

Perhaps the stakes in this situation weren't terribly high, but sometimes they are. Things don't always go our way. We make mistakes and fail to get the job done. The way we treat ourselves in these situations matters.

When people I know and love are being especially hard on themselves, I like to ask: "If your best friend were in this exact situation, what advice would you offer?"

Most people would offer empathy, understanding, and suggestions for self-care. For many of us, it seems easier to be Honest, Kind, and Forgiving with others than it is with ourselves.

Research on these character strengths points to why we should turn them inward.

Honesty is being true to oneself and authentic with others; taking responsibility for one's feelings and actions.[2] According to a 2012 study, telling fewer lies is linked with closer relationships, better physical health, and less stress and sadness.[3]

Kindness is valuing and helping others with no expectation of reciprocity.[4] Kindness turned inward is also known as self-compassion. Self-compassion is known to buffer anxiety, self-criticism, perfectionism, and boost goal mastery, optimism, and social connectedness.[5]

Forgiveness is accepting the shortcomings of others and giving them a second chance.[6] Forgiveness is important in repairing and reconciling relationships and keeps us from harmful ruminations about the wrong others do to us.[7] It

Treating yourself with Honesty, Kindness, and Forgiveness is not only the right thing to do, it's also good for you.

can also apply to the wrong we do to ourselves. We can be our own worst critics and even knowingly harm our health and relationships. It's easy to hold on to resentment and anger for the choices we make.

Being human means allowing ourselves to make mistakes and learning from them. If you tend to expect more from yourself than others, try turning your character strengths inward. You can do this with Fairness, Love, Curiosity, and other strengths. Today, though, start with Honesty, Kindness, and Forgiveness.

Today's Activity*

1. Think of a recent situation when you made a mistake or were overly critical of yourself.

2. How can you take responsibility for your actions or feelings (Honesty)?

3. How can you accept what happened and give yourself a second chance (Forgiveness)?

4. How can you care for or nourish yourself mentally, emotionally, or physically (Kindness)?

5. Extend all three strengths toward yourself today.

Today's Reflection and Writing Prompt

Character strengths turned inward empowered me to be...

*Adapted from Character Strength Intervention (CSI) 13 in *Character Strengths Interventions: A Field Guide for Practitioners* by Ryan Niemiec.

Day 24

Shift a bad habit

Many years ago, my weekdays as a single working parent typically began in a mad dash to get the day started. I would wake up, shower and get dressed, wake the kids up, make sure they were dressed/fed/packed for the day, find my keys, leave and lock up, come back for whatever we forgot, lock up again, drop the kids off at the sitter's house, and head to the train. No matter how much preparation I did the night before, I always felt rushed. I chalked it up to living the life of a single mom.

Being a single working parent comes with an overflowing plate. Although I had many habits that helped me manage all the priorities, some didn't serve me well. For instance, I typically went to bed too late and ate high-carb breakfasts on-the-go. I didn't stop to think about how these habits led to less energy and a bad mood.

Consider the following excerpt from Niemiec's book *Character Strengths Interventions*:

> *"We mindlessly eat snacks…(a habit of behavior), watch hours of television…(a habit of behavior), and replay the same worry-prone scenarios (a habit of mind) as tension arises. Our autopilot mind has taken over and flies our habits wherever our mind wishes to go."*[8]

As I grew older and wiser, I learned that by focusing on my habits I could identify which ones weren't serving me well. I could also change the ones I had complete control over, like when I go to bed and what I eat. Today, I usually go to bed at a reasonable time and eat a healthy breakfast because I feel better when I do so.

Looking back, I see the character strengths that I used to improve my habits. I used Self-regulation to catch myself in

Your character strengths can help you train your autopilot mind to go in a new direction.

unwanted behaviors, Judgment to analyze and choose a preferred behavior, and Teamwork with accountability buddies to help make positive changes stick.

Recently, I discovered another bad habit. As I sat down at my desk each morning, I noticed feeling unsettled and often anxious. This habit set a negative tone to my work day and started a downward spiral. You'll see what I mean as I peel back the layers, using today's activity, in the table that follows.

Habit: Feeling unsettled and anxious at the beginning of my work day.

First Task: Review emails	What was I thinking?	What was I feeling?
Before reviewing emails	"I'm not able to finish many tasks, such as (named them all in my mind)." Why can't I finish simple tasks in a timely fashion?" "I should have spent time on ____ instead of ____."	Anxious Tense Not very capable
While reviewing emails	"Look at all the new tasks and deadlines being added to my plate." "My list never shrinks, just grows."	More anxious and tense Overwhelmed by details Even less capable
After reviewing emails	"I dread this. I better get going…I have a lot to do." "Why can't I finish…"	Unmotivated Deflated Resigned

No wonder I felt tense and anxious! My autopilot mind was flying me into darkness and hyperbole. It wasn't true that I couldn't finish tasks in a timely manner. I had many examples that demonstrated otherwise. It also wasn't true that my list only grew and never shrank. That was an exaggeration.

This was an especially embarrassing discovery because I often work successfully with clients to manage and take control of their priorities and schedules, yet I hadn't taken control of my own. Once I understood what was happening, I was able to scc a mindful and strength based way forward. I started with a Mindful Pause.

If you recall from Day 22, the Mindful Pause helps:

1.   short-circuit worry, stress, and autopilot thinking

2.   take advantage of present moment awareness

3.   activate character strengths in the moment

4.   shift your mindset to mindfulness and character strengths[9]

What a wonderful tool, and how well-matched to this situation!

I took a Mindful Pause, and the character strength that came up was Fairness. I certainly wasn't being Fair to myself or setting myself up for success. I accomplished things, but I wondered how much more I could accomplish and how much more engaged I could feel.

My thoughts and feelings were unfair and not even true. I began to see how other strengths could help me. Honesty to acknowledge these harmful thoughts and feelings. Forgiveness to accept them and have the freedom to move on. Creativity to think of a more energizing way to start my day. Hope to envision a different routine.

My new routine emerged from this process. I began each day with a Mindful Pause and envisioned how I could use the strength throughout my day. Sometimes I would journal about it. As I started my work day with a Mindful Pause, I felt buoyed by a positive shift in my thinking and feelings. That motivated me to add more strength-based activities to my daily habit.

Over time, rather than berating myself for not completing everything, I celebrated progress and the completion of milestones. Instead of dreading new tasks, I envisioned

> Use your strengths to envision a positive habit, practice the habit, and stay committed to your practice.

exciting new possibilities. When obstacles arose, I thought of ways my character strengths would help manage them. I had trained my autopilot mind to go in a new direction.

I continue to feel more productive and confident. Not every day is perfect, but I'm not striving for perfection. When I skip a day, I realize how much I miss my practice and feel motivated to return to it the next day.

This isn't an easy or intuitive process. However, by becoming more mindful of your habits, you can retrain your autopilot mind to move away from habits that don't serve you well and towards strength-based habits that do.

Today's Activity

1. Choose a bad habit, something you are bothered by, that you do nearly every day. Perhaps you stay up too late or snap at colleagues and family members each time they approach you. Start small.

2. What is your first task in the habitual routine? Be clear on where the habit begins.

3. The next time you engage in that task, ask yourself what happens before, during, and after. What do you think? How do you feel? Create a grid like the sample I shared.

4. Describe a more positive habit that will serve you well. Perhaps you'd like to begin going to bed by 10:00 pm. Or taking a few deep breaths before you encounter a certain person at work. Start small.

5. Take a Mindful Pause and allow a character strength to enter your awareness. How can this strength help you shift your habit?

6. Put your new habit into practice. Notice what other strengths can help you stay committed to it.

Today's Reflection and Writing Prompt

Strengthening a bad habit was…

Day 25

See conflict through a lens of strengths

A friend was telling me about her daughter's upcoming wedding. I could sense her excitement as she talked about her future son-in-law, the wedding, the reception, and family and friends who would be part of the celebration.

She was also feeling a bit anxious about getting everything done in time and about not getting along with her husband, who was concerned about practical matters like the expenses.

We decided to look at the conflict through a lens of strengths. From her perspective, he was not on board and being difficult throughout the planning process. She felt there was a growing rift in their relationship because of this wedding.

Sometimes, relationship conflicts are rooted in strengths collisions, overuse, or underuse on the part of one or both parties. You're already familiar with collisions, overuse, and underuse from Week 3.

I asked if any strengths could be colliding. She realized that there were. Her signature strength Appreciation of Beauty and Excellence was in high gear, driving her and her daughter's choices for flowers, food, venue, and invitations. Simultaneously, her husband's signature strength, Prudence, was sounding the alarm bell about breaking the budget with mounting expenses.

She also noticed instances of overuse and underuse. Her underuse of Gratitude for not expressing appreciation for his hard work at monitoring the expenses and earning the income. His underuse of Kindness in the way he communicated about the finances.

Strengths collisions, overuse, and underuse can contribute to conflicts. Communicating in the language of strengths can open the door to new solutions.

105

As we began to see grievances through a lens of strengths, there was the palpable shift of a burden being lifted. She seemed relieved to see this marital strain through a clear and positive lens of strengths rather than the murky blame of weaknesses.

"So how can you reconnect with your husband and work together instead of against one another?" I asked.

She decided to express her signature strength, Gratitude, to him for caring about the family finances and for being such a good provider in general. To her surprise he responded in Gratitude, saying he was Grateful to be able to provide in this way.

It was a moment of connection and clarity that led to many others. She was reminded of the qualities she values and appreciates in her husband. She was also reminded that using a strengths lens can shift an interaction and a relationship.

This process is not meant to replace therapy or to resolve issues of a deeper nature. In some cases, working with a qualified professional might be necessary. However, when you're not getting along with someone, especially someone important to you, using a lens of strengths rather than one of blame can help you understand the nature of the conflict and strengthen the relationship.

Today's Activity

1. Think of someone with whom you disagree on a particular issue. Choose a small issue before trying something larger. Perhaps your parent is constantly on your back for not making your bed. Or your office mate constantly interrupts you in your office. Choose a small conflict you're likely to be engaged with today. Try to clearly describe the situation.

> Using a strengths lens can shift the trajectory of a difficult conversation and lead you back to what's best about the other person.

2. Name the strengths collisions, overuse, and underuse, both on your part and his or hers.

3. Notice which strengths can help you work together or approach the situation in a new way.

4. Which of your strengths can you express more openly? Which of your strengths might you tone down?

5. When the situation arises, put your strengths to work and notice what happens.

Today's Reflection and Writing Prompt

When I applied a strengths lens to a difficult situation, the result was…

Day 26

Live your strengths daily

Did you ever have one of those days when time flies by and at the end of the day you wondered what you did all day? If you stopped to think about it, you'd notice the hundreds, probably thousands, of tasks that add up to your day.

Some tasks are probably repetitive chores, like doing the laundry. Others are tasks you probably look forward to, like meeting a friend for lunch. Some feel like obligations, while others feed your soul. Some involve connecting with people, others are solo. Some are required, others optional. Some pertain to home, hobbies, work, school, or volunteer settings.

Washing dishes is one task I find completely mundane. I'd like to avoid doing them, but I don't like when dishes pile up in the sink. Still, applying my signature strengths can boost my energy, pleasure, and meaning. For instance, I can engage:

- Humor and Creativity, both signature strengths, to make dish soap "suds sculptures"
- Kindness, a signature strength, to clean up the dishes *before* someone asks me to
- Love, a middle strength, to reflect on the last time I did the dishes with my son or daughter

Engaging strengths, I get a burst of pleasure and meaning, even in a mundane activity like washing dishes. My character strengths are the pathways.

Aligning character strengths with work tasks can be just as powerful. Following is an example of a person with signature strengths Gratitude and Judgment. He aligns these strengths with two different tasks: grocery shopping and closing his biggest deal at work.

> Aligning your character strengths with virtually every daily activity is likely to boost your energy, pleasure, and performance.

Aligning Strengths With Daily Activities

Task	Gratitude	Judgment
Grocery shopping (home/chore)	1. Thank store employees who manage, stock, clean, and other people I encounter in the store. 2. Appreciate others in the grocery supply chain – those who grow, manufacture, transport, plan etc. 3. Appreciate the variety and abundance of healthy foods available to me.	1. Evaluate and choose options for different food items based on highest nutritional content. 2. Be open to buying a vegetable I've never tried, just because studies show health benefits.
Closing biggest deal in career (work/aspirational goal)	1. Express appreciation for this opportunity in an appropriate manner. 2. Appreciate the many skills, experiences, mentors, and resources that led me to this moment.	1. Before the negotiation begins, consider all views /details of the deal, not just the ones that are important to me. Open my vision to include details I might not otherwise consider.

By aligning his signature strengths with daily activities, he's likely to boost meaning, engagement, pleasure, and achievement.

Aligning your strengths with daily tasks is a relatively straightforward process, but it takes time and practice to groom the habit. Try it and notice how you can align your signature strengths with *all* your daily activities.

Today's Activity*

1. Think of two different kinds of tasks you will complete today.

2. How will your signature strengths add meaning, joy, engagement, or connection with others? Write down the strengths and how you will employ them.

3. If it's helpful, draw and fill in a grid like the one offered.

4. Feeling fueled by your strengths, complete your tasks.

Today's Reflection and Writing Prompt

When I aligned my signature strengths with daily tasks, I experienced....

*Adapted from Character Strength Intervention (CSI) 20 in *Character Strengths Interventions: A Field Guide for Practitioners* by Ryan Niemiec.

Day 27

Ignite goals and overcome obstacles

On Day 26, you aligned signature strengths with both a mundane and an engaging task. You can apply a similar process to nearly every situation you encounter in life to benefit yourself and others.

You can also apply your strengths to other complex tasks, like achieving long-term goals. The research on setting and reaching goals goes back at least fifty years and clearly shows that having and working toward goals contributes to success.[10]

When you reflect on your achievements, how many of them directly aligned with your strengths, interests, and values? These are considered self-concordant goals, typically geared to accomplishing dreams, fulfilling purpose, and leading a meaningful life. In a lecture on self-concordant goals, Tal Ben-Shahar described them as goals that are freely chosen by you.

Becoming a lawyer might be a self-concordant goal if you feel passionately about injustices in the world and strive to correct them. On the other hand, becoming a lawyer might not be self-concordant if you are simply following in your parents' footsteps or desire to earn a good living.

When goals are self-concordant, your chances of attaining them and enjoying the journey increase. Today, you will identify a self-concordant goal. Perhaps you wish to deepen your connection with a romantic partner because you've been traveling a lot and miss him or her. Perhaps you want to relax more because your stress level has been high and it's impacting your mood or health.

Whether you seek to relax more, connect more deeply with someone, or achieve another meaningful goal, your strengths can assist you in the ways you've practiced in this book.

A simple process for choosing a meaningful goal and aligning strengths follows.

1. What do you want to accomplish? (the goal)

2. Why? (the importance)

3. How will you get there? (the action steps)

4. What obstacles are you likely to encounter along the way? (the roadblocks to success)

5. How can your strengths help? (making the journey productive and meaningful)

Below is an example of someone whose goal is to relax more.

What I Want to Do/Goal	What strengths might help me?
Relax more.	Love of Learning to research health benefits of relaxation. Appreciation of Beauty and Excellence to spend more time in nature. Potentially all 24 character strengths.
Why/Importance I can't enjoy time with friends because my stress levels are so high. Our friendships go back a long time. We love each other and enjoy spending time together.	Gratitude to appreciate these friendships.
I would like to have more energy for activities and people I care about.	Love to show I care. Zest to energize myself.
How I Will Get There/Action Steps 1. Meditate for 5 minutes daily.	Prudence to plan it into my schedule each day. Creativity to brainstorm how to use my time on a day off.
2. Unplug from technology for 24 hours each week.	Hope to envision the benefits of unplugging.
Obstacles Too much to do.	Temper overuse of Perseverance with a signature strength.
Stressed at the thought of being unplugged all day.	Judgment to analyze priorities. Forgive myself; recognize that I'm human. Turn Kindness inward when feeling anxious.

This framework reflects not only identifying the goal but envisioning potential obstacles and naming how your strengths increase the likelihood of success. This question of how your strengths can help is key.

If you've completed Days 1 through 26, you've already been exposed to many ways your strengths can help. For instance:

- Use a signature strength in new ways
- Turn a strength inward
- Elevate a middle or lower strength
- Temper an overused strength
- Amplify an underused strength
- Appreciate and value the best in yourself (spot strengths)
- Take a Mindful Pause
- Deploy a specific character strength:
  - Use Perseverance
  - Express thanks and Gratitude
  - Extend an act of Kindness
  - Smile and show your Love
  - Create something new
  - Learn something new
  - Be Curious and ask questions
  - Surround yourself in the Beauty and Excellence in nature

What others can you think of? Today's activity will give you practice choosing the practices that fit with your specific goal, action steps, and obstacles. You might discover that it's more motivating to pursue challenging goals when strengths are engaged and supported in the process.

Today's Activity

1. Think of a meaningful goal you'd like to accomplish in the next month. Start small before going bigger.

2. Draw a grid like the one offered and fill in the blanks.

3. Complete one action step.

Today's Reflection and Writing Prompt

Today's activity prompted me to…

Day 28

Review Week 4

This week you practiced living your strengths and doing more of what you do best. As a quick review you:

- Practiced the Mindful Pause, a tool to circumvent worry and shift you into your strengths on Day 22.
- Turned Honesty, Kindness, and Forgiveness inward on Day 23.
- Shifted a bad habit into a positive one on Day 24.
- Applied a lens of strengths to a difficult situation on Day 25.
- Infused your daily activities with strengths on Day 26.
- Took a step toward a meaningful goal on Day 27.

You're nearing the final stretch. Great work!

Congratulations! Well done! Remember that your strengths are a place to come home to. A place where you can be comforted and nourished. A place to be who you are and do what you do best.

We began this week with a quotation:

> *"Breathing in, I see my strengths.*
>
> *Breathing out, I value my strengths.*
>
> *Dwelling now in my strengths,*
>
> *I express myself fully."*

Which activities from Week 4 helped you dwell in your strengths?

Today's Activity

1. Choose one of this week's activities and repeat it.

2. Practice the Strengths Gatha, synchronizing your breath in and out with each line. Repeat the gatha often throughout the day.

Today's Reflection and Writing Prompt

Dwelling now in my strengths, I...

THE CLOSING DAYS

Welcome to the closing days!

You're approaching the finish line, and I want to help you finish strong. This involves looking back at what you've already accomplished and then looking forward with all your strengths engaged. On day 29, you'll review your journey, notice what went well, and celebrate your accomplishments. On day 30, you'll shift your attention to the future so that you can decide how to continue.

Enjoy these closing days.

Day 29

Celebrate best moments

> *"Don't cry because it's over, smile because it happened."*
>
> —Dr. Seuss

Reflecting on your accomplishments can help you consolidate what you've learned.

This quotation from renowned children's book author, Dr. Seuss, makes me smile. In fact, I'm smiling now. I can't stop smiling because I know that Day 29 is all about reflection and celebration.

If you completed Days 1 through 28, you've covered a considerable amount of ground. Well done! If you took more than 28 days to complete these activities, welcome to the club! It takes both willpower and commitment to practice. Life intervenes; willpower wanes; old habits and the autopilot mind take over. Returning to the practice and beginning again without judging yourself is the key to your staying power.

If you completed fewer than 28 days, I salute you too. Well done! We are each on our own journey, and each journey begins with one step. If you have taken one step, perhaps you'll take another. Then another. I encourage you to keep trying, taking small steps forward, and returning to the practice over and over until it becomes part of a supportive and affirming routine.

To recap Weeks 1 through 4:

- In Week 1 you embarked on a journey of exploration to develop a meaningful awareness of your strengths.

- In Week 2 you spotted and appreciated strengths in action by observing yourself and others, even people you don't know or care for!

- In Week 3 you developed a more nuanced strengths practice by focusing on strengths overuse, underuse, and balanced use; strengths collisions; and strengths that cultivate happiness and achievement.

- In Week 4 you practiced living your strengths and doing more of what you do best.

You have explored many facets of character strengths. You have acquired knowledge and tools. You have experienced how your strengths are pathways to happiness and success. Today's activity is about reflecting on this journey, mining your experiences for best moments, and celebrating them.

A best moment is any memorable moment when you felt positive, confident, accomplished, or inspired, such as:

- **An insight** when exploring a strength or noticing how you put it into action
- **Increased awareness** about why you are the way you are and how you express yourself when at your best
- **A discovery** of something new about yourself or a loved one
- **Greater appreciation and acceptance** of what's best about you or someone else
- **An accomplishment,** such as resolving a conflict with a partner, making progress on an important goal, or improving a bad habit
- **The experience of heightened positive emotions** such as joy, pride, hope, or gratitude when using a signature strength or tempering an overused strength
- **Self-compassion,** perhaps for the first time in a long time
- **The act of making someone else's day** when spontaneously spotting strengths in him or her
- **A positive shift within yourself, a situation, a relationship, or your day** caused by using a strengths lens

These are simply examples. Only you can define a best moment for yourself.

Recall some of your best moments, re-live and savor the positive experiences, and carry them with you as you go forward.

119

I'd like to share one of my best moments while writing this book. Midway through the writing process, as I dedicated more time to writing I began to feel lonely and isolated. These feelings grew, and I admit that I thought about quitting. Other personal matters were taking priority, and it seemed too hard to continue.

I completed what is now Day 27, *Ignite Goals and Overcome Obstacles*. Doing so brought immense clarity to the importance of finishing, the obstacles I faced, and the strengths I needed to keep going. The clarity was game-changing. My strengths were pathways to the finish line. To celebrate, I engaged Zest, dancing and singing to my favorite songs; Kindness, giving myself time off when I needed it; and Appreciation of Beauty and Excellence, enjoying walks in nature.

How do you like to celebrate? Give it some thought as you begin today's activity.

Today's Activity

1. Take time to reflect on your strengths practice. Review your notes or thumb through the daily practices to jog your memory.

2. What are your best moments? Write them down. Post them in a place where you'll see them frequently or carry them with you as a reminder of your strengths.

3. What would be a good way to celebrate your hard work? Whether you think you accomplished a little or a lot, use your strengths to celebrate.

Today's Reflection and Writing Prompt

How have I changed? What do I do differently? My strengths practice helped me become…

Day 30

Craft a future fueled by strengths

"To choose is to create your reality."

—Tal Ben-Shahar

In one of his positive psychology lectures, Tal Ben-Shahar said that people who make intentional choices rather than rely on luck, fate, or "laws of attraction" are generally happier, more resilient, and more successful.

Choosing strengths is one of those choices. On Day 1, you chose to begin or not. Each day leading to this point, you made choices to complete the activity or to skip it, to do part of the activity or all of it.

> Living your strengths is a lifelong journey of choices, discovery, and growth.

Now you're faced with another choice regarding what comes next. Will you choose to continue a strengths practice? Try something else? Go back to the habits you had before?

I hope you'll continue your strengths practice because it is a lifelong journey of learning and growth. There are infinite ways to take your practice forward. You can simply repeat the 30 days using different strengths and situations. You can complete any days that you missed. Or you might wish to:

- Take a deep dive into one or two strengths you'd like to feel more confident about.
- Practice strengths-spotting each day.
- Practice the optimal level of strengths use in difficult situations.
- Set a meaningful goal and use your strengths to support action steps and overcome obstacles.
- Incorporate the Mindful Pause into your routine.

Set yourself up for success as you go forward.

Below are a few tips to help you go forward:

1. Decide realistically how much time you'd like to commit. Your practice can be short and simple, such as sending a daily Gratitude text to a loved one or taking a Mindful Pause each day. Or it can be longer and more complex, such as creating a strength-based habit.

2. Choose a practice that resonates with you in some way. It should support your health, relationships, work, or other important part of your life.

3. Forgive yourself when you miss a day, or 3 days, or 10 days, and use Self-regulation to return your attention to your practice.

4. Keep your practice flexible and fresh. If it begins to feel stale, go back to steps 1 and 2. Notice what would be more meaningful and actionable.

5. Set reminders for yourself to practice until the habit becomes ingrained. Set an alert on your phone, use sticky notes in prominent places, or place reminders in your calendar. One of the hardest things about a new practice is remembering to do it.

6. Work with a trusted friend or professional to boost accountability. A professional who regularly works with strengths can help you deepen your practices.

7. Consider your practice a lifelong journey rather than an event that begins and ends.

I wish you much success as you decide what happens next. Accompanying you on this journey has been my pleasure. I leave you with the words of Tal Ben-Shahar, based on his book *Choose the Life You Want.*

> *"At every moment, you have a choice – now, a minute from now, 10 years from now. These moments add up to a lifetime; these choices add up to a life. Your life."*

May you continue to make choices that shift you toward the person you wish to become and what you'd most like to do with all your remaining days.

Today's Activity

1. Choose one or more practices to continue and the amount of time you will commit.

2. Set up an accountability system for yourself.

3. Tomorrow, begin to create your new reality.

Today's Reflection and Writing Prompt

As I decide how to live a strengths-based life, I'm looking forward to…

To Be Continued…

I have a confession to make: I don't like to say goodbye. At the end of Day 30 when I said, "Accompanying you on this journey has been my pleasure," it definitely felt like a goodbye. I had a visceral reaction. I get that feeling when something naturally concludes and I realize I don't want it to end.

The good news is that this can be a new beginning. Some who have reviewed this book prior to publication said they'll use it as a resource with clients, their management teams, children, grandchildren, and friends. Others said they will use it to continue focusing on their own strengths.

Let the ripple effect grow!

If you continue with your study and practice of character strengths, perhaps you're interested in:

1. Receiving updates on strengths research and practice
2. Connecting with a community of strengths practitioners for support or accountability
3. Working 1:1 to focus even more on living your strengths
4. Planning how to take strengths to your team, your family, or community

I'd love to help you take your strengths to the next level! To stay connected, email me at Jane@StrengthBasedLiving.com or go to my website at www.StrengthBasedLiving.com to read about my latest updates.

Remember that living your strengths is a journey. I like the phrase "to be continued" to describe the next leg of the journey. It opens the door to new possibilities without dismissing difficult feelings about endings.

It's officially time to part ways, and I feel Hopeful about the possibility of new adventures together.

To be continued…

References

Before You Begin

1   VIA Institute (n. d.). Frequently Asked Questions. Retrieved from http://www.viacharacter.org/www/About-Institute/FAQs?QuestionID=69&AFMID=592

2   Cooperrider, D. L. (2012). The concentration effect of strengths: How the whole system "AI" summit brings out the best in human enterprise. *Organizational Dynamics*. DOI: http://dx.doi.org/10.1016/j.orgdyn.2012.01.004

3   Peterson, C., & Seligman, M. E. P. *(2001). How can we allow character to matter?* Impact Portal, Ross School of Business. Retrieved from http://www.bus.umich.edu/facultyresearch/research/TryingTimes/Character.htm

4   Niemiec, R. M. (2014). *Mindfulness and character strengths: A practical guide to flourishing.* Boston, MA: Hogrefe Publishing, p. 35.

5   Lavy, S., & Littman-Ovadia, H. (2016). My better self: Using strengths at work and work productivity, organizational citizenship behavior and satisfaction. *Journal of Career Development*, 1-15. DOI: 10.1177/0894845316634056.

6   Weber, M., & Ruch, W. (2012b). The role of a good character in 12-year-old school children: Do character strengths matter in the classroom? *Child Indicators Research, 5*, 317-334.

7   Fung, B. K. K., Ho, S. M. Y., Fung, A. S. M., Leung, E. Y. P., Chow, S. P., Ip, W. Y., … & Barlaan, P. I. G. (2011). The development of a strength-focused mutual support group for caretakers of children with cerebral palsy. *East Asian Archives of Psychiatry, 21*, 64-72.

8   Hanson, R., (2017, June 01). Take in the good. Retrieved from http://www.rickhanson.net/take-in-the-good/

9   Baumeister, R. F., Bratslavsky, E., Finkenauer, C., & Vohs, K. D. (2001). Bad is stronger than good. *Review of General Psychology, 5*, 323-370. doi:10.1037//1089-2680.5.4.323

10   Doidge, N. (2010). *The brain that changes itself: Stories of personal triumph from the frontiers of brain science.* New York: Penguin Books, p. 242.

11   Lally, P., van Jaarsveld, C. H. M., Potts, H. W. W. & Wardle, J. (2010). How are habits formed: Modelling habit formation in the real world. *European Journal of Social Psychology, 40*, 998–1009. doi:10.1002/ejsp.674

12   Metzgar C. J., Preston, A. G., Miller D. L. & Nickols-Richardson S. M. (2015). Facilitators and barriers to weight loss and weight loss maintenance: A qualitative exploration. *Journal of Human Nutrition and Dietetics.* 28, 593-603. doi:10.1111/jhn.12273

13   Stringer, L. (2016, June 09). The essential ingredient you're missing in achieving your goals. *Huffington Post.* Retrieved from https://www.huffingtonpost.com/entry/the-essential-ingredient-youre-missing-in-achieving-your-goals_us_5730ecc3e4b016f37896af06

Week 1: Exploring Your Best Self

1   Seligman, M. E. P. (2011). *Flourish*. New York: Free Press. p. 38-39.

2   Crabb, S. (2011). The use of coaching principles to foster employee engagement. *The Coaching Psychologist, 7,* 27-34.

3   Madden, W., Green, S., & Grant, A. M. (2011). A pilot study evaluating strengths-based coaching for primary school students: Enhancing engagement and hope. *International Coaching Psychology Review, 6,* 71-83.

4   Linley, P. A., Nielsen, K. M., Gillett, R., & Biswas-Diener, R. (2010). Using signature strengths in pursuit of goals: Effects on goal progress, need satisfaction, and well-being, and implications for coaching psychologists. *International Coaching Psychology Review, 5,* 6-15.

5   Gander, F., Proyer, R. T., Ruch, W., & Wyss, T. (20123). Strength-based positive interventions: Further evidence for their potential in enhancing well-being. *Journal of Happiness Studies,* 14, 1241-1259.

6   Beard, A. (2014, May). Leading with humor. *Harvard Business Review.* https://hbr.org/2014/05/leading-with-humor

7   Welsh, J. (2011, September 14). Why laughter may be the best pain medicine. *Scientific American.* Retrieved from https://www.scientificamerican.com/article/why-laughter-may-bethe-best-pain-medicine/

8   Wellenzohn, S., Proyer, R., Ruch, W., (2016). Humor-based online positive psychology interventions: A randomized placebo-controlled long-term trial. *The Journal of Positive Psychology,* 11, 584-594.

9   Peterson, C., & Seligman, M. E. P. (2004). *Character strengths and virtues: A handbook and classification.* New York: Oxford University Press, p. 28.

10   Niemiec, R. M. (2017, February 13). Rise Up: The hidden power of your phasic strengths. *Psychology Today Online.* Retrieved from https://tinyurl.com/PowerPhasicStrengths

11   Grant, A. M., & Schwartz, B. (2011). Too much of a good thing: The challenge and opportunity of the inverted U. *Perspectives on Psychological Science,* 6, 61-76. https://doi.org/10.1177/1745691610393523

12   Crabb, S. (2011). The use of coaching principles to foster employee engagement. *The Coaching Psychologist, 7,* 27-34.

Week 2: Connecting & Building Relationships

1   Seligman, M. E. P., Steen, T. A., Park, N., & Peterson, C. (2005). Positive psychology progress: Empirical validation of interventions, *American Psychologist,* 60, 410–21.

2   Niemiec, R. M. (2014). *Mindfulness and character strengths: A practical guide to flourishing.* Boston, MA: Hogrefe Publishing, p. 28.

3 Peterson, C., & Seligman, M. E. P. (*2001*). *How can we allow character to matter?* Impact Portal, Ross School of Business. Retrieved from http://www.bus.umich.edu/facultyresearch/research/TryingTimes/Character.htm

4 Niemiec, Ryan, M. (2014). *Mindfulness and character strengths: A practical guide to flourishing.* Boston, MA: Hogrefe Publishing, p. 90.

Week 3: Boosting Your Confidence & Competence

1 Biswas-Diener, R. & Dean, B. (2010). *Practicing positive psychology coaching: Assessment, activities, and strategies for success.* Hoboken, NJ: John Wiley & Sons Inc., p. 34.

2 Niemiec, R. M. (2014). *Mindfulness and character strengths: A practical guide to flourishing.* Boston, MA: Hogrefe Publishing, p. 89.

3 Freidlin, P., Littman-Ovadia, H., & Niemiec, R. M. (2017). Positive psychopathology: Social anxiety via character strengths underuse and overuse. *Personality and Individual Differences, 108,* 50-54. DOI: dx.doi.org/10.1016/j.paid.2016.12.003

4 Niemiec, R. M. (2014). *Mindfulness and character strengths: A practical guide to flourishing.* Boston, MA: Hogrefe Publishing, p. 29.

5 Biswas-Diener, R., Kashdan, T. B., & Minhas, G. (2011). A dynamic approach to psychological strength development and intervention. *The Journal of Positive Psychology, 6,* 106-118.

6 Miller, C. A. (2017). *Getting grit: The evidence-based approach to cultivating passion, perseverance, and purpose.* Boulder, CO: Sounds True Inc., p. 170.

7 Park, N., & Peterson, C. (2009). Character strengths: Research and practice. *Journal of College and Character, 10,* 1-10.

8 Wagner, L., & Ruch, W. (2015). Good character at school: Positive classroom behavior mediates the link between character strengths and school achievement. *Frontiers in Psychology.* doi: 10.3389/fpsyg.2015.00610

9 Littman-Ovadia, H., & Lavy, S. (2016). Going the extra mile: Perseverance as a key character strength at work. *Journal of Career Assessment, 24,* 240–252. http://doi.org/10.1177/1069072715580322

10 Money, K., Hillenbrand, C., & Camara, N. D. (2008). Putting positive psychology to work in organizations. *Journal of General Management, 34,* 21-26.

11 Niemiec, R. M. (2013, November 27). The 5 happiness strengths. Retrieved from https://www.psychologytoday.com/blog/what-matters-most/201311/the-5-happinessstrengths.

12 Simon, H. B. (n.d.). Giving thanks can make you happier. *Harvard Health Publishing.* Retrieved from https://www.health.harvard.edu/healthbeat/giving-thanks-can-make-you-happier

13 Buschor, C., Proyer, R. T., & Ruch, W. (2013). Self- and peer-rated character strengths: How do they relate to satisfaction with life and orientations to happiness? *Journal of Positive Psychology, 8*, 116-127.

14 Seligman, M. E. P. (2011). *Flourish.* New York: Free Press, p. 84.

15 VIA Blog (2015, December 11). Hopeful for what's to come. Retrieved from http://www.viacharacter.org/blog/hopeful-for-whats-to-come/

16 Peterson, C., Park, N., Hall, N. and Seligman, M. E. P. (2009). Zest and work. *Journal of Organizational Behavior*, 30: 161–172. doi:10.1002/job.584

Week 4: Living Your Strengths

1 Niemiec, R. M. (2018). *Character strengths interventions: A field guide for practitioners.* Boston, MA: Hogrefe Publishing, Character Strengths Intervention (CSI), p. 65.

2 Peterson, C., & Seligman, M. E. P. (2004). *Character strengths and virtues: A handbook and classification.* New York: Oxford University Press, p. 249.

3 HuffPost Wellness (2012, August 7). Honesty linked with better health: Study. Retrieved from https://www.huffingtonpost.com/2012/08/07/honesty-healthy-lies-truth_n_1748144.html

4 Peterson, C., & Seligman, M. E. P. (2004). *Character strengths and virtues: A handbook and classification.* New York: Oxford University Press, p. 326.

5 Niemiec, R. M. (2018). *Character strengths interventions: A field guide for practitioners.* Boston, MA: Hogrefe Publishing Corporation, Virtue: Humanity/Spotlight On Kindness.

6 Niemiec, Ryan M. (2018). *Character strengths interventions: A field guide for practitioners.* Boston, MA: Hogrefe Publishing Corporation, Virtue: Temperance/Spotlight On Forgiveness.

7 Worthington, E. (n.d.). Everett Worthington Research. Retrieved from http://www.evworthington-forgiveness.com/research/

8 Niemiec, R. M. (2018). *Character strengths interventions: A field guide for practitioners.* Boston, MA: Hogrefe Publishing Corporation, CSI 68.

9 Niemiec, R. M. (2018). *Character Strengths Interventions, A Field Guide for Practitioners.* Boston, MA: Hogrefe Publishing Corporation, CSI 65.

10 Locke, E. A. (1968) Toward a theory of task motivation and incentives. *Organizational Behavior and Human Performance*, 3, 157-189, https://doi.org/10.1016/0030-5073(68)90004-4.

CHARACTER STRENGTHS OVERUSE & UNDERUSE

CHARACTER STRENGTH	ESSENCE	OVERUSE	UNDERUSE
Appreciation of Beauty and Excellence	Sense of awe for beauty, excellence, skill	Perfectionistic, snobbery	Oblivious, lack of wonder
Bravery	Facing fears, speaking up for what's right	Foolhardy risk-taker	Coward
Creativity	Originality, adaptive	Eccentric	Conformity
Curiosity	Seeking novelty and new experiences	Nosy	Uninterested
Fairness	Unbiased, adherence to principles	Detached	One-sided, partisan
Forgiveness	Letting go	Permissive	Merciless
Gratitude	Thankful, appreciative	Ingratiated	Entitled
Honesty	Authenticity, integrity	Righteous	Insincere
Hope	Positive future-mindedness	Negative	Wearing rose-colored glasses
Humility	Modesty	Self-deprecation	Baseless self-esteem
Humor	Playful, light-hearted	Giddy	Overly serious
Judgment	Critical, rational thinking	Narrow minded, cynical	Unreflective
Kindness	Caring and helping	Intrusive	Uncaring, indifferent
Leadership	Positively influencing others	Dictatorial	Compliant
Love	Valuing close relationships	Uninhibited emotionally	Isolated
Love of Learning	Mastery, adding new knowledge	Know-it-all	Complacent
Perseverance	Industrious	Obsessive	Idle, apathetic
Perspective	Seeing the broader view	Overbearing	Shallow
Prudence	Careful, planful	Rigid, stuffy	Risk-seeking, throwing caution to the wind
Self-Regulation	Disciplined	Inhibited	Self-indulgent
Social Intelligence	Tuned in to others	Over-analyzing	Clueless
Spirituality	Connecting with purpose and meaning	Fanatic	Lack of purpose or ideals
Teamwork	Collaborative	Dependent	Selfish
Zest	Vital, enthusiastic	Hyperactive	Sedentary

This table is based on definitions from the VIA Classification of Character Strengths and Virtues and the Character Strengths Overuse and Underuse worksheet from R.M. Niemiec's book *Mindfulness and Character Strengths* © 2014 Hogrefe Publishing (used with permission).

Made in the USA
Lexington, KY
13 December 2018